PATHWAYS TO RESILIENCE

FRAGILE AND CONFLICT-AFFECTED SITUATIONS AND SMALL ISLAND DEVELOPING STATES APPROACH ACTION PLAN, 2026–2030

ASIAN DEVELOPMENT BANK

6 ADB Avenue, Mandaluyong City, 1550 Metro Manila, Philippines
Tel +63 2 8632 4444; Fax +63 2 8636 2444
www.adb.org

ISBN 978-92-9277-806-4 (print); 978-92-9277-807-1 (PDF); 978-92-9277-808-8 (ebook)
Publication Stock No. SPR260198-2
DOI: http://dx.doi.org/10.22617/SPR260198-2

Notes:
In this publication, "$" refers to United States dollars.
All photos by ADB.

Cover design by Rommel Marilla.

CONTENTS

TABLES, FIGURES, AND BOXES

TABLES

FIGURES

BOXES

ACKNOWLEDGMENTS

The preparation of this Fragile and Conflict-Affected Situations (FCAS) and Small Islands Developing States (SIDS) Approach Action Plan, 2026–2030 was led by Lainie Thomas together with Joana Custoias, Jogendra Ghimire, Ursula Lagan, and Rangina Nazrieva, as well as consultants Alanna Inserra, Gervic Laurio, and Junica Soriano, with guidance from Ben Graham. The FCAS and SIDS Unit of the Fragility and Engagement Division provided regular feedback and valuable inputs.

This Action Plan could not have been prepared without the support and contributions of many staff members from departments across Asian Development Bank, including directors general, country directors, regional heads of operation coordination, country operations heads, and country economists from FCAS-classified developing member countries and SIDS; Budget, Personnel, and Management Systems Department teams working on benefits, training and staffing; Procurement, Portfolio, and Financial Management Department teams working on procurement in the Pacific and financial management; Office of Business Intelligence and Operations Coordination staff; Private Sector Operations Department teams working on the Pacific; policy and results teams in Strategy, Policy, and Partnerships Department; and staff working in FCAS and SIDS contexts from the sectors departments and from the climate change, adaptation, disaster risk management, environment, and regional cooperation divisions.

Staff in resident missions and Pacific country offices provided invaluable feedback, as did Board members.

Support on coordination and administration matters was provided by Heidi Renacia and Romana Sevilla. Samantha Brown edited the manuscript, and the Department of Communications and Knowledge Management facilitated publication.

ABBREVIATIONS

ABAS	–	Antigua and Barbuda Agenda for SIDS
ADB	–	Asian Development Bank
ADF	–	Asian Development Fund
CCFE	–	Fragility and Engagement Division
CRF	–	Corporate Results Framework
DMC	–	developing member country
FCAS	–	fragile and conflict-affected situations
FRA	–	fragility and resilience assessment
FSA	–	FCAS and SIDS Approach
KAA	–	key action area
MDB	–	multilateral development bank
MTR	–	midterm review
NOM	–	new operating model
PSD	–	private sector development
SDG	–	sustainable development goal
SFA	–	strategic focus area
SIDS	–	small island developing states
TA	–	technical assistance
TOC	–	theory of change
US	–	United States

EXECUTIVE SUMMARY

From Fragility to Resilience: Action Plan, 2026–2030

The Asian Development Bank (ADB) remains steadfast in its commitment to support its most vulnerable developing member countries (DMCs), particularly (i) those fragile and conflict-affected situations (FCAS) and (ii) small island developing states (SIDS). In 2021, ADB approved the FCAS and SIDS Approach (FSA) to operationalize differentiated approaches to improve the effectiveness and results of ADB assistance in these contexts.

Action Plan, 2026–2030 renews and updates the initial 5-year action plan (2021–2025) under the FSA, building on implementation experience, the midterm review of the FSA, and extensive internal and external consultations. It refines implementation priorities and institutional actions to respond to evolving development, operational, and geopolitical contexts. The ADB President approved the Action Plan, 2026–2030 on March 12, 2026.

Rising Fragility

Since the approval of the FSA, the development context in Asia and the Pacific has become more complex and volatile. Fragility has intensified globally and in the region, driven by compounding shocks, including climate change and disasters, conflict and displacement, geopolitical fragmentation, fiscal stress, and structural vulnerabilities. FCAS and SIDS are disproportionately exposed to these risks while often having the least capacity to manage and mitigate them.

Over this period, ADB's engagement in FCAS and SIDS has expanded significantly. Financing volumes have increased, portfolios have become larger and more complex, and expectations for results—particularly in resilience, private sector development, regional cooperation, and digital transformation—have grown. At the same time, delivering results in these contexts remains challenging. Project performance reflects persistent capacity constraints, weak project readiness, governance challenges, and overall difficult operating environments.

Action Plan, 2026–2030 responds to these realities. It consolidates and streamlines actions from Action Plan, 2021–2025, carries forward the FSA's theory of change and three institutional pillars, and sets out a refreshed, practical set of actions for 2026–2030 that emphasize coherence, flexibility, resilience, and better results. The directions and actions reflect extensive consultations and inputs from staff across ADB and other stakeholders.

Progress Since 2021

Implementation of the FSA and the initial action plan was generally effective—a good start on which to build. Progress was made across all three pillars. Under Pillar 1, ADB introduced greater flexibility in procurement, financial management, and nonsovereign operations; expanded concessional financing options for FCAS and SIDS; piloted faster approaches for small nonsovereign transactions; and utilized novel modalities to maintain engagement in de facto government contexts.

Under Pillar 2, ADB strengthened its organizational focus on FCAS and SIDS; expanded staff training and peer learning; increased field presence; and deepened operational and knowledge partnerships. Under Pillar 3, fragility and resilience assessments and related diagnostics were developed, piloted, and applied to inform country programming and operations, while advancing work to modernize the FCAS classification system.

Despite these gains, reviews and consultations highlight persistent gaps between policy intent and operational reality, underscoring the need for sharper, more consistently applied differentiated approaches.

What Action Plan, 2026–2030 Delivers

Action Plan, 2026–2030 sets actions to strengthen ADB's engagement and results in FCAS and SIDS and specific institutional actions under the three FSA pillars to guide ADB's work through 2030. Together, these aim to move ADB's engagement from managing fragility toward building resilience.

ADB will focus on interlinked priorities including: scaling up and refining financing, particularly for adaptation, disaster risk management, crisis response, and displacement; reforming and strengthening the operational delivery model; strengthening private sector development and other strategic focus areas, such as digital transformation, which can serve as a crosscutting enabler for resilience; transforming approaches to capacity development; enhancing partnerships and coordination; and building staff capabilities.

Under Pillar 1, ADB will further streamline and differentiate business processes across sovereign and nonsovereign operations, including in procurement, financial management, safeguards, project design, and monitoring, with an emphasis on speed and flexibility. Under Pillar 2, actions focus on attracting and retaining skilled staff, expanding field presence, strengthening learning pathways and peer networks, enhancing knowledge products, and improving portfolio monitoring and reporting. Under Pillar 3, actions will deepen the use of multidimensional diagnostics, strengthen early warning and risk monitoring, update the FCAS classification system as a management tool, and more systematically apply analytical findings to country strategies and project design.

Alignment, Implementation, and Monitoring

The plan aligns with the Strategy 2030 Midterm Review, Corporate Results Framework, 2025–2030, and strategic focus areas—in particular those of resilience and empowerment. It also informs and complements other directional documents, including the forthcoming Pacific Approach.

Effective implementation will require ADB-wide ownership and action. While many actions can be undertaken within existing processes, others will require process adjustments or changes.

The FCAS and SIDS Unit will continue to coordinate, support, and monitor implementation, reporting progress annually through the FSA Annual Report. Progress will be tracked using action-level monitoring and disaggregated Corporate Results Framework indicators.

Actions will be refined as circumstances evolve.

I. INTRODUCTION

Developing member countries face increasingly complex challenges. These challenges span economic, social, political, environmental, demographic, institutional, and geopolitical dimensions that directly impact development prospects and progress in the region. Understanding these dynamics is imperative to the effective design and implementation of Asian Development Bank (ADB) policies and operations. This is especially important in fragile and conflict-affected situations (FCAS), small island developing states (SIDS), and subnational pockets of fragility and conflict, where delivering development results has been most challenging.[1]

ADB remains steadfast in its support for vulnerable countries and contexts. In its Charter, ADB pledges to pay *special regard* to the needs of its smaller and less-developed member countries, recognizing their unique situations.[2] Over the decades, it has strengthened this commitment and, in Strategy 2030, made an explicit pledge to apply *differentiated approaches* in FCAS and SIDS.[3] Following this, ADB approved its FCAS and SIDS Approach (FSA),[4] which built on an earlier operational plan for FCAS.[5] This Action Plan, 2026–2030, builds on the midterm review (MTR) of the FSA's initial implementation period and reflects findings from desk reviews and analyses, internal and external consultations, and other inputs.[6]

1 Following a harmonized system adopted by multilateral development banks in the early 2010s, ADB continues to classify countries as FCAS if (i) the average rating of its country performance assessment and the World Bank's country policy and institutional assessment is less than 3.2 and/or (ii) a United Nations peacekeeping and/or peacebuilding mission has been present in the country in the previous 3 years. ADB updates its FCAS classification every 2 years, with the last one taking place in 2024. Sixteen DMCs self-identify as SIDS. Thirteen DMCs are currently classified as FCAS, 10 of which are also SIDS (Kiribati, the Marshall Islands, the Federated States of Micronesia, Nauru, Niue, Papua New Guinea, Solomon Islands, Timor-Leste, Tuvalu, and Vanuatu), plus Afghanistan, Lao People's Democratic Republic, and Myanmar. The six other SIDS (non-FCAS classified) are Cook Islands, Fiji, Maldives, Palau, Samoa, and Tonga. ADB's regular assistance to Afghanistan has been on hold since 15 August 2021, but the bank has supported the basic needs of the Afghan people since 2022 through a special arrangement with United Nations agencies. Similarly, ADB's regular assistance to Myanmar has been on hold since 1 February 2021, with ADB providing support for basic human needs through United Nations agencies.

2 Asian Development Bank (ADB). 1965. *Agreement Establishing the Asian Development Bank*.

3 ADB. 2018. *Strategy 2030: Achieving a Prosperous, Inclusive, Resilient, and Sustainable Asia and the Pacific*.

4 ADB. 2021. *Fragile and Conflict-Affected Situations and Small Island Developing States Approach*.

5 ADB. 2013. *Operational Plan for Enhancing ADB's Effectiveness in Fragile and Conflict-Affected Situations*.

6 ADB. 2024. *Summary of Midterm Review: Fragile and Conflict-Affected Situations and Small Island Developing States Approach*.

Differentiated approaches remains a fundamental guiding principle. The theory of change (TOC) underlying the FSA holds that applying differentiated approaches will result in better-designed and delivered operations, which ultimately lead to long-term sustainable development (Appendix 1).[7] While differentiated approaches are now a widely recognized principle, their coherence and application need strengthening internally and in developing member countries (DMCs). Three pillars underpin the TOC and guide ADB's institutional focus and work on FCAS and SIDS: (i) improving the responsiveness of standard ADB processes, procedures, and practices; (ii) increasing institutional capacity for operations in these contexts; and (iii) enhancing diagnostics and understanding of these contexts.[8]

Achieving better results will require improvements in key areas. While the performance of ADB-financed operations in FCAS and SIDS shows some improvement over time, it continues to lag ADB's overall results. This reflects not only the challenging operational contexts but also the need for ADB to further strengthen its support while, at the same time, step up efforts to improve country capacities and the broader enabling environment for development.

The plan supports resilience and empowerment and other institutional priorities. It supports ADB's strategic focus areas, in particular resilience and empowerment, and also addresses climate action, private sector development, regional cooperation and public goods, and digital transformation in the context of FCAS and SIDS. It aligns with ADB's new policy architecture, categorized as *management guidance*, providing guidance on operation or technical matters, without creating new binding obligations on ADB or DMCs.[9] ADB will review and update the FSA in 2030 and seek management approval for a new approach and action plan.

The plan reaffirms and sets new actions under the FSA. Reviews and consultations on progress made on the FSA and its first 5-year action plan (2021–2025) provide the basis for this plan. It carries forward the underlying TOC and principal elements of the original FSA and sets out a refreshed set of actions toward 2030, reflecting the evolving external and internal contexts and a wide range of inputs. Detailed actions under the three pillars are in Appendix 2 and Appendix 3. The actions were discussed and validated through extensive consultations and feedback.

7 Aiming to enhance responsiveness and improve results, the working definition of *differentiated approach* is a new or different way of doing business in certain contexts, such as in FCAS-classified DMCs and SIDS. This may include adaption, customization, and/or the distinct application of standard business processes and procedures to suit unique contexts. Doing business differently commonly involves innovation, new ways of working, the use of purpose-made financing instruments and modalities, strategic partnering and collaboration, and other tailored solutions.

8 ADB's accomplishments under the FSA are listed in the summary of its MTR (footnote 6), and in its annual reports.

9 ADB. 2024. *Asian Development Bank's Policy Architecture.*

II. EVOLVING CONTEXTS

Fragility and Development Trends

Progress is stalling on Sustainable Development Goals. Given the persistent and compounding challenges slowing development, including the major setbacks brought about by the coronavirus disease pandemic, nearly all countries are unlikely to achieve most of the Sustainable Development Goals (SDGs) by 2030. Only a handful of indicators show improvement, while data gaps hamper monitoring and effective interventions.[10] Against the global backdrop of slowing development progress, FCAS and SIDS face even bigger barriers towards progress.

Fragility is rising globally and in Asia and the Pacific. Pervasive and diverse shocks and stresses drive rising fragility.[11] Standard ADB diagnostics and assessments of fragility typically focus on key dimensions of vulnerability and fragility, including structural, environmental, economic, political, societal, and institutional dimensions. The latest *States of Fragility* global report defines the current era as one characterized by multiple crises and high uncertainty.[12] Compounding factors driving this fragility include socioeconomic stresses, climate change, disasters as a result of natural hazards, environmental degradation, and political and geopolitical dynamics, among other factors. These dimensions of fragility are also observed at the subnational level in some DMCs not currently classified as FCAS by ADB. Growing numbers of displaced persons and conflict-related fatalities in the region, with rates in the most recent decade exceeding those in the previous decade, contribute to the rising fragility.[13]

[10] UN Economic and Social Commission for Asia and the Pacific. 2025. *Asia and the Pacific SDG Progress Report 2025: Engaging Communities to Close the Evidence Gap*.

[11] ADB uses the Organisation for Economic Co-operation and Development (OECD) definition of fragility: *a combination of (i) exposure to risk; and (ii) insufficient coping capacity of the state, system, or community to manage, absorb, or mitigate those risks*, as introduced in OECD. 2016. *States of Fragility: 2016*.

[12] Organisation for Economic Co-operation and Development (OECD). 2025. *States of Fragility: 2025*.

[13] Displacement represents one indicator of fragility that can underscore the scale and human impact of risk. Across ADB DMCs, at the end of 2024 there were 10.1 million internally displaced persons due to conflict and violence, while there were 19.2 million internal displacements due to disasters during the same year.

Box 1: Development Progress in Fragile and Conflict-Affected Situations and Small Island Developing States: Relatively Lower and Slower

States that are more fragile (i) see slower development progress over time, (ii) are more sensitive to downside risks and shocks, and (iii) take longer to recover from such shocks, relative to less fragile states. Comparing fragile and conflict-affected situations and small island developing states to all other Asian Development Bank (ADB) developing member countries across four broad measures—economic growth, human development, tax administration, and internet access—illustrates this.

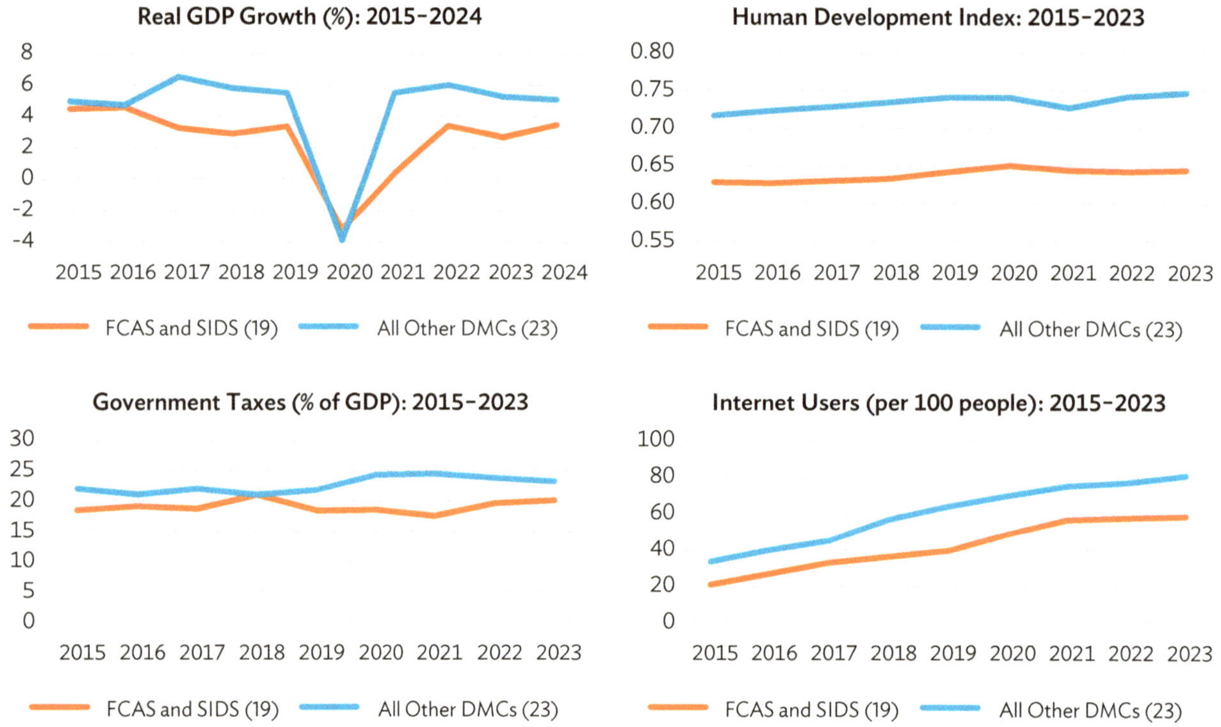

DMCs = developing member countries, FCAS = fragile and conflict-affected situations, GDP = gross domestic product, SIDS = small island developing states.

Note: Figures are based on median values of the respective indicators for each country group and year; only years for which sufficient data are available for each indicator and country group are shown.

Source: ADB.

FCAS and SIDS are disproportionately impacted. FCAS and SIDS face high and growing exposure to multidimensional and compounding risks, yet have limited capacities to manage and mitigate these risks. This makes the achievement of SDGs all the more challenging. In FCAS, governance and institutional capacity; economic, political, and social stability; peace and security; and vulnerability to the effects of climate change and natural hazards remain prevalent factors affecting development. Furthermore, these impacts are wide-ranging. For example, climate and disaster risks affect public administration through payroll discontinuity, procurement delays, displacement of staff, and budget reallocation pressures. SIDS face similar challenges, in addition to remoteness and dispersion, small populations and markets, narrow-based economies, and fiscal and economic management challenges. While these challenges impact all DMCs to some degree, their effects on FCAS and SIDS are more pronounced, resulting in lower and slower development progress (Box 1).

Private sector development has been mixed but shows some progress. FCAS and SIDS face clear structural barriers that constrain private sector investment and development. Nonetheless, ongoing analysis of private sector development (PSD) trends in SIDS, drawing on a broad range of indicators, provides useful insights and optimism. This covers quantitative and qualitative measures of (i) enabling environments for investment and (ii) investment and growth patterns.[14] A handful of SIDS have managed to improve both their enabling environments, as measured by incremental changes in policy and regulatory conditions, and accessibility and reliability of basic infrastructure and services. Steady improvements in electricity, shipping, digital technology, communication, e-government, and mobile money connectivity over the past 2 decades suggest that, despite the structural barriers, enabling environments can be broadly strengthened. Meanwhile, data on actual private sector investment and growth over time show a much more mixed and volatile picture.

Many other challenges prevail. Other concerning developments include geopolitical unpredictability; increased militarization; debt sustainability challenges; resurgence of border disputes, demographic pressures, including out-migration; and shifts in development financing. In the Pacific, political dynamics (national, regional, and geopolitical) have shaped and influenced cooperation and development. Gender imbalances in decision-making and governance are extreme in some FCAS and SIDS, as is gender-based violence. Non-SIDS face serious development challenges (Box 2). Numerous non-FCAS-classified DMCs have pockets of fragility characterized by chronic poverty and subnational conflict.

Climate challenges and natural hazards amplify vulnerability. Climate impacts and disasters triggered by increased natural hazards amplify existing vulnerabilities and create new pathways for instability, conflict, economic and forced displacement, as well as loss of livelihoods and income. Rising sea levels, more intense tropical cyclones, prolonged droughts, coastal erosion, and geophysical hazards such as earthquakes directly threaten lives, infrastructure, ecosystems, and economies. However, disaster risk analytics play an increasing role in informing adaptation, infrastructure planning, and disaster preparedness decisions in FCAS and SIDS. For SIDS and many other DMCs, the consequences of sea-level rise alone will be catastrophic, forcing the displacement of communities, undermining food and water systems, and placing a disproportionate burden on those least equipped to adapt. While climate shocks and environmental disasters jeopardize hard-won development gains across all DMCs, for some DMCs—most critically the world's four atoll nations,[15] all of which are ADB members—slow-onset climate events, especially sea-level rise, pose significant risks to habitation and sovereignty. More proactive planning and preparation for transformational adaptation is urgent; planning must follow for addressing displacement, planned relocation, and migration.

Emerging opportunities also present risk. The energy transition and rapid adoption of digital technology, including artificial intelligence, are opportunities but also sources of evolving uncertainty and risk in their potential to cause economic, environmental, and social disruption and discontent. Key risks include land competition and environmental impacts of critical minerals' exploration and extraction, which can also influence pathways for instability, conflict, corruption, and displacement. Rapid technological change may deepen the digital divide and cause labor market disruption, impact social cohesion, and exacerbate gender inequalities and demographic pressures. In fragile contexts, these pressures are expected to deepen preexisting inequalities, strain public institutions, and heighten social and political tensions where governance and economic capacity are already limited (footnote 12). Without targeted, adaptive, agile, and forward-looking interventions, these dynamics may undermine community resilience, erode trust in institutions, and exacerbate the fragility risks facing vulnerable populations (footnote 12).

[14] CCFE analytics on *Private Sector Development in Small Island Developing States: Current State and Key Trends from 2005 to 2024* (available upon request).

[15] The four atoll nations are Kiribati, Maldives, the Marshall Islands, and Tuvalu. Atolls comprise low-lying coral islands that encircle a central lagoon, formed through the growth of coral reefs around sinking volcanic islands.

Box 2: ADB's Largest FCAS: A Brief Situation Report

Afghanistan,[a] Myanmar,[b] and Lao People's Democratic Republic (PDR) are the Asian Development Bank's (ADB) three fragile and conflict-affected situations (FCAS)-classified developing member countries (DMCs) that are not small island developing states (SIDS). They face distinct, severe challenges.

Lao PDR is preparing to graduate from "least developed country" status in late 2026, but its economy remains fragile. External debt, at $14.1 billion in 2025, was 94% of gross domestic product. Inflation was 7.7%, brought down with tight monetary and fiscal policies from 23.1% in 2024. Nearly 39% of youth are not in education, employment, or training. While digital foreign exchange reforms and export rules have stabilized its currency and reserves, the impending "graduation cliff" threatens access to preferential trade arrangements and concessional financing. Climate change adds further risk by reducing water levels of the Mekong River, jeopardizing hydropower revenues crucial for debt servicing.

Myanmar remains engulfed in widespread armed conflict and a humanitarian crisis. Over 3.5 million people are internally displaced, with about 1.6 million displaced people from Myanmar and asylum-seekers in the region, including around 1.18 million in Bangladesh and 136,000 in Thailand.

Meanwhile, Afghanistan struggles to survive under severe governance and economic challenges under the de facto authorities. Declining humanitarian aid is heavily impacting the 23 million people needing assistance. Border tensions and rising displacement due to both conflict and disasters triggered by natural hazards are a significant concern. Women and girls face severe restrictions, with 2.2 million girls out of school—a figure expected to grow. The continued influx of returning refugees and displaced people further compounds existing challenges and increases needs on the ground, including over 2.3 million Afghans from Iran and Pakistan arriving since the beginning of 2025.[c] These overlapping economic, social, and political crises in ADB's largest FCAS-classified DMCs underscore the fragility and complexity of transitions.

[a] ADB placed its regular assistance to Afghanistan on hold effective 15 August 2021, with ADB providing support for basic human needs through United Nations agencies.

[b] ADB's regular assistance to Myanmar has been on hold since 1 February 2021, with ADB providing support for basic human needs through United Nations agencies.

[c] United Nations Development Programme. 2025. *From Return to Rebuild for Afghan Returnees and Host Communities*.

Source: ADB.

Digital transformation is a crosscutting enabler. Connectivity, cybersecurity, digital public infrastructure, and data systems underpin the FSA, serving as foundational enablers of resilience, institutional capacity, and service delivery in low-capacity and fragile settings. Their potential to support capacity development, enhance administrative transparency, connect dispersed populations, and facilitate service provision could be transformative. Yet many FCAS and SIDS do not have the foundations to harness these opportunities or manage and mitigate the associated risks.

Varying Development Financing Trends

Project portfolios in SIDS have steadily expanded in the last decade. The portfolios of projects in SIDS supported by development finance partners have evolved and expanded in terms of annual disbursements as well as the number of active aid providers and their projects, based on recent analysis (Figure 1).[16] Several important points stand out. Annual disbursements peaked at

[16] This analysis draws on the International Aid Transparency Initiative (IATI) database. IATI is a global multi-stakeholder program that promotes transparency and standardized reporting of aid flows to developing countries to better plan and coordinate resources. It includes over 1,800 reporting organizations of various types.

Figure 1: Development Finance Trends in SIDS: 2015–2024

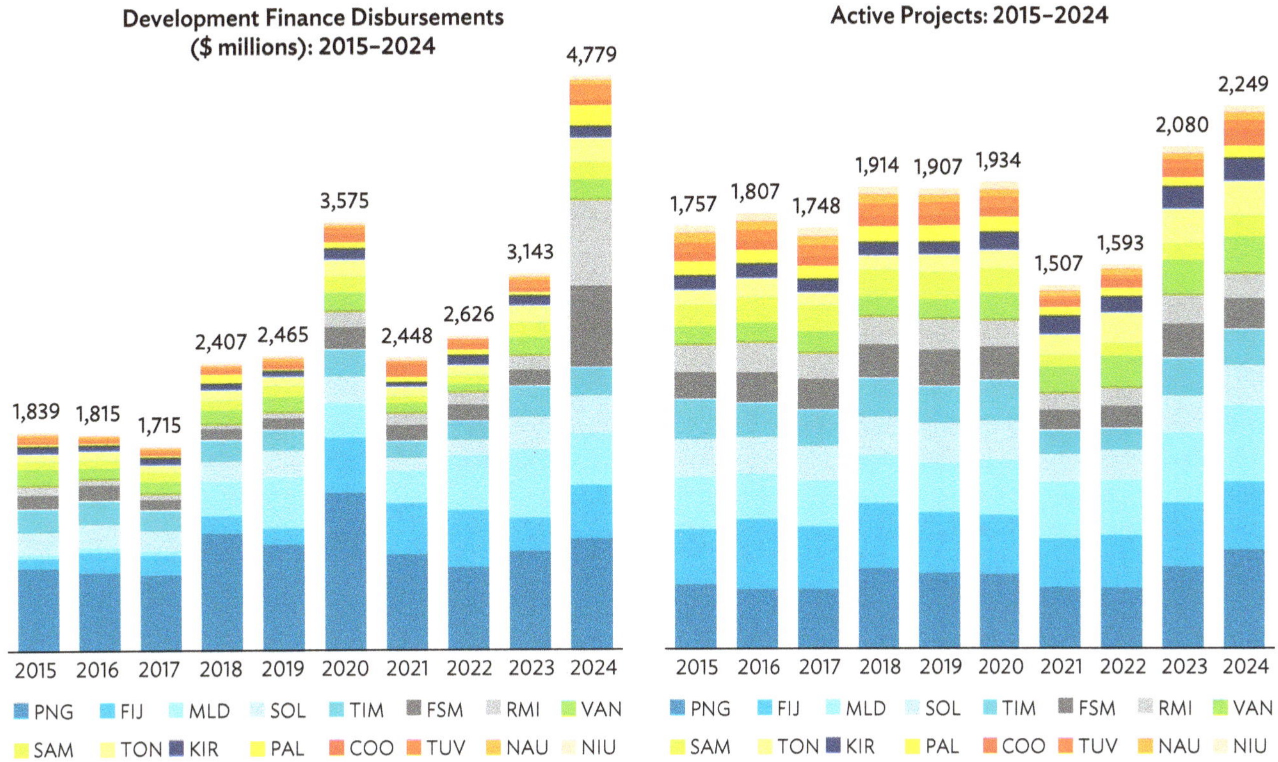

COO = Cook Islands, FIJ = Fiji, KIR = Kiribati, MLD = Maldives, RMI = Republic of the Marshall Islands, FSM = Federated States of Micronesia, NAU = Nauru, NIU = Niue, PAL = Palau, PNG = Papua New Guinea, SAM = Samoa, TIM = Timor-Leste, TON = Tonga, TUV = Tuvalu, VAN = Vanuatu.

Source: Analysis based on International Aid Transparency Initiative data up to calendar year 2024 (accessed 4 October 2025).

$3.6 billion in 2020 during the height of the pandemic, subsequently reverted to pre-pandemic levels, and resumed their upward trajectory in 2023–2024. The sharp rise in 2024 was driven by upfront disbursements made under the renewed Compacts of Free Association between the United States (US) and the Marshall Islands, the Federated States of Micronesia, and Palau.

Meanwhile, the number of active aid projects (i.e., those which had disbursements) has also steadily risen each year, from just under 1,800 to over 2,000, with a dip in 2021–2022 during the pandemic (Figure 1). Also, the number of active providers rose from just over 40 in 2015 to 63 as of 2024, with the numbers peaking at 70 or more during most of 2018–2023. Except for Niue, which joined ADB in 2019, ADB is among the top five development partners for all of these SIDS based on total disbursements made during the 2015–2024 period.

Development financing to the larger FCAS-classified countries has been mixed. Over the same 2015–2024 period, annual aid flows to the Lao People's Democratic Republic (Lao PDR) steadily increased from around $300 million to over $500 million. In Afghanistan,[17] annual disbursements declined from over $10 billion in 2015 to under $4 billion in 2024. For Myanmar,[18] the trend is somewhat mixed but annual disbursements have generally remained at around $1 billion.[19] Annual disbursements from the US show a steady decline, with preliminary data for 2025 suggesting a sharp downturn.

[17] ADB placed its regular assistance to Afghanistan on hold effective 15 August 2021, with ADB providing support for basic human needs through United Nations agencies.

[18] Effective 1 February 2021, ADB placed a temporary hold on sovereign project disbursements and new contracts in Myanmar.

[19] International Aid Transparency Initiative. Country Development Finance Data (accessed 4 October 2025). The UN Financial Tracking Service reported $458 million in humanitarian funding in 2024.

Refreshed SIDS Agendas

SIDS adopted an ambitious new agenda in 2024. At the fourth Global SIDS Conference in Antigua and Barbuda in 2024,[20] all SIDS, including the 16 SIDS members of ADB, adopted a new 10-year sustainable development agenda, the Antigua and Barbuda Agenda for SIDS (ABAS).[21] ABAS emphasizes that the next decade will be critical for SIDS in addressing systemic vulnerabilities while enabling resilient and prosperous futures. ABAS sets out pathways to address structural vulnerabilities in SIDS and priorities for the international community to better partner with SIDS on these efforts. The agenda focuses on transforming the unique vulnerabilities of island nations into opportunities through four pillars: building resilient economies; safe, healthy, and prosperous societies; a secure future; and environmental protection and sustainability.

SIDS seek further reforms in international finance institutions. ABAS calls for reforms to international finance institutions—including ADB—to ensure SIDS' priorities are better represented and their unique development circumstances fully addressed. Many are updating their approaches (Appendix 4). This should happen through enhanced access to concessional finance, including both concessional loans and grants; adequate resources for SIDS to invest in climate resilience, disaster risk reduction, and sustainable development; and direct support for disaster response through resilient infrastructure and faster post-disaster financial support.

New agendas guide development in the Pacific. Adopted by Pacific leaders in 2022, the 2050 Strategy for the Blue Pacific Continent aims to ensure a resilient, secure, and prosperous future for the region through a unified regional response to shared challenges.[22] The strategy emphasizes reforms to improve regional architecture and calls for more effective collaboration with major development partners in the Pacific. The vision is a resilient region of peace, harmony, security, social inclusion, and prosperity where all Pacific peoples lead free, healthy, and productive lives. Other plans and initiatives underpin these Pacific priorities, like the Pacific Regional Framework on Climate Mobility[23] and the 2023 Pacific Resilience Facility.[24]

20 ADB was represented by the Pacific Department and Climate Change and Sustainable Development Department.
21 United Nations. 2024. *Fourth International Conference on Small Island Developing States: The Antigua and Barbuda Agenda for SIDS (ABAS)—A Renewed Declaration for Resilient Prosperity*.
22 Pacific Islands Forum. 2022. *2050 Strategy for the Blue Pacific Continent*.
23 Pacific Islands Forum. 2023. *Pacific Regional Framework on Climate Mobility*.
24 Pacific Islands Forum. Pacific Resilience Facility.

III. REVIEW OF ADB SUPPORT FOR FCAS AND SIDS

This section presents a summary of the reviews and consultations on ADB's implementation of the FSA and the 2021 Action Plan in order to inform plans for 2026–2030.

Review of the FSA and 2021 Action Plan

Implementation of the FSA and 2021 Action Plan was satisfactory. A 2023–2024 MTR of the FSA's initial implementation found that the approach remained relevant and implementation was generally effective (footnote 6). The MTR concluded that the three pillars and the TOC remain suitable in terms of guiding institutional responsiveness to FCAS and SIDS, despite changes to the internal and external operating environments. The MTR recommended that the FSA continue as the institutional approach for FCAS and SIDS, but that a new FSA Action Plan 2026–2030 be developed, in line with the MTR of Strategy 2030 and other institutional developments.[25]

Access to finance and business processes have improved (Pillar 1). Under Pillar 1 of the FSA, which focused on improving the responsiveness of processes and procedures, ADB revised business processes and templates to facilitate differentiated approaches, while preparing guidance notes on applying existing flexibilities in FCAS and SIDS contexts (footnote 8). ADB undertook a number of procurement initiatives targeting FCAS and SIDS.[26] ADB streamlined nonsovereign transactions by introducing a faster approach to small nonsovereign transactions[27] and piloting the ADB Frontier and Wayfinder Program[28] to help increase nonsovereign

[25] ADB. 2024. *Strategy 2030 Midterm Review: An Evolution Approach for the Asian Development Bank*.

[26] Examples include an FCAS and SIDS Procurement Guidance Note; increased procurement staffing in SIDS; targeted knowledge products; and embracing quality-based evaluation methods and local participation criteria.

[27] ADB. 2022. *Enhanced Faster Approach to Small Nonsovereign Transactions (FAST)*. This is a streamlined approach to enhance efficiency for high-impact and higher-risk small nonsovereign deals by delegating approval authority to the President under Board-approved criteria, simplifying pre-Board procedures, and providing annual reporting to the Board on their implementation and performance.

[28] ADB. 2025. *ADB Wayfinder (Pacific) Program Under the Enhanced Faster Approach to Small Nonsovereign Transactions Policy*. This program is aimed at providing tailored financing and risk-sharing to support early-stage and underserved businesses in frontier markets, particularly Pacific SIDS. It is designed as a de-risking, blended-finance facility to unlock private investment in high-cost and high-risk markets.

Table 1: Budgeted Staff Positions in FCAS and SIDS Field Offices, 2020–2025

Item	2020	2021	2022	2023	2024	2025
Total	**97**	**111**	**110**	**109**	**119**	**131**
RM-owned	71	85	85	82	51	57
Outposted	26	26	25	27	68	74

FCAS = fragile and conflict-affect situations, RM = resident mission, SIDS = small island developing states.

Note: AS7 positions have been included in the staff count for 2020–2024 to be comparable to 2025, which is inclusive of AS7, pursuant to the new job architecture. Count includes both international and national staff, and both resident mission-owned positions and outposted staff.

Source: ADB.

operations in FCAS and SIDS. ADB increased its Asian Development Fund (ADF) 14 resource envelope for FCAS and SIDS through country allocations (with an expanded economic vulnerability premium for SIDS), the community development window for Afghanistan (footnote 17) and Myanmar (footnote 18), and continued preferential access to the thematic window. ADB also introduced new concessional lending terms for SIDS and allowed small DMCs a larger limit of contingent disaster financing. Lastly, ADB utilized novel financing arrangements to provide support to the people of Afghanistan and Myanmar through UN agencies, given the de facto government situation in both countries.

Institutional capacity for working in FCAS and SIDS strengthened (Pillar 2). In June 2023, under ADB's New Operating Model (NOM), the bank established an FCAS and SIDS Unit to coordinate FSA implementation with support from a working group and departmental focal points. To boost staff capacity for working in FCAS and SIDS contexts, ADB offered introductory and advanced training, which more than 250 ADB staff completed. A peer learning network with over 200 members facilitates knowledge exchange among staff to share experiences. ADB developed knowledge products on FCAS and SIDS contexts, which were disseminated through reports, blogs, newsletters, and webinars. ADB also established and expanded knowledge and operational partnerships to further expand its knowledge and deepen coordination.

Staffing in FCAS and SIDS has increased. ADB increased staff positions in FCAS and SIDS field offices, with international and national positions increasing by 35% from 2020 to 2025, which exceeds the 28% average staff increase across ADB field offices over the same period. Excluding Afghanistan and Myanmar Resident Missions, whose numbers were affected by the situations in those countries, the increase is 78%. This includes field-based positions and outposted staff (Table 1). The increase is mainly attributed to additional financial management and procurement officers; outposting of energy, health, and transport specialists; and placement of additional environmental and social safeguard officers in the field. Placements included additional staff in Solomon Islands and Timor-Leste, while outpostings went to Fiji and Papua New Guinea. In 2025, ADB appointed a country director to the new Solomon Islands Resident Mission and an advisor for the North Pacific, and began preparations for a new North Pacific office. The NOM, which entailed staff moving from regional departments and resident missions to sectors and other departments, affected the 2023 and 2024 numbers.

Also, as part of the NOM, several resident mission-owned national staff positions were mapped to support functions such as procurement, financial management, and safeguards. While these national staff positions were retained in field offices, position ownership was mapped to groups such as Procurement, Portfolio, and Financial Management Department and the Office of Safeguards. The new mapping creates more agile and responsive field offices with more outposted positions, but may create the perception that RMs have lost staff through the NOM.

New diagnostics have been developed and applied (Pillar 3). ADB enhanced its understanding of DMC contexts through fragility and resilience assessments

Figure 2: ADB FCAS and SIDS Portfolio (sovereign, nonsovereign, sector): 2016 and 2025

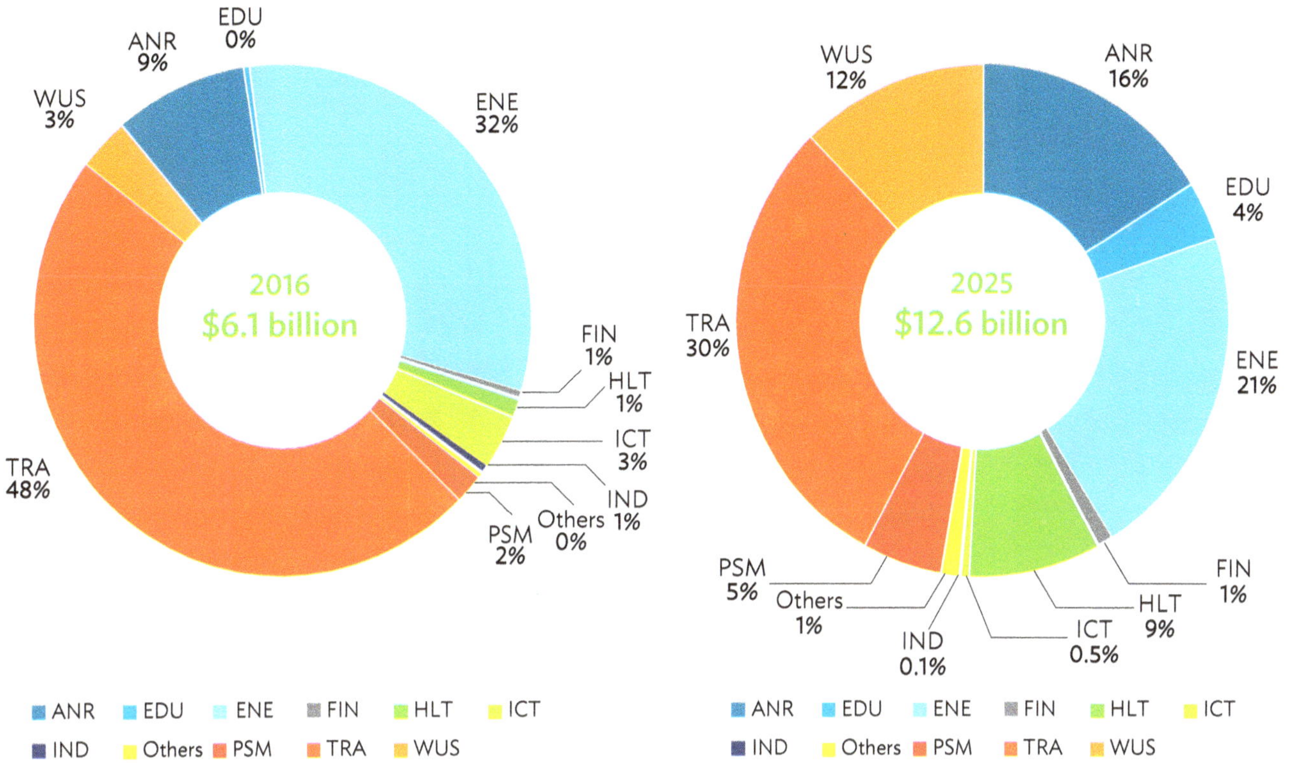

ANR = agriculture, natural resources, and rural development; EDU = education; ENE = energy; FIN = finance; HLT = health; ICT = information and communication technology; IND = industry and trade; PSM = public sector management; TRA = transport; WUS = water and other urban infrastructure and services.

Source: ADB.

(FRAs), which are diagnostic tools that identify and analyze risk, vulnerability, and fragility, and propose resilience actions to inform country partnership strategies and project-level design. Other diagnostic tools developed and applied at the national and subnational levels include watching briefs for enhanced situational understanding; political economy analyses; and political risk assessments that update ADB Management on relevant and evolving country issues, including during conflict and crisis situations (including non-FCAS and SIDS contexts). Diagnostic assessments and analyses include broad-based consultations and engagement with civil society organizations, other nonstate actors, and minority groups. A country risk monitor under development will track evolving risks across a range of indicators in DMCs and serve as a potential early warning system for emerging economic, financial, political, social, and other crises. ADB's ongoing work to update its FCAS classification system, moving from a static binary system to a more nuanced and multidimensional spectrum approach that better reflects fragility across all ADB DMCs, will help focus attention and resources on commensurate resilience-strengthening responses.

ADB Operations Performance and Lessons

Sovereign operations have grown rapidly, nonsovereign operations less so. ADB has been responsive in scaling up sovereign resources for FCAS and SIDS, primarily through successive ADF replenishments (Appendix 5). From 2016 to 2025 the sovereign portfolio grew from $5.8 billion (84 projects) to over $12.2 billion (163 projects). The nonsovereign portfolio grew more modestly, from $273 million (6 projects) to $450 million (13 projects) (Figure 2).

Figure 3: Projects with Priority Components, 2012–2018 and 2019–2025

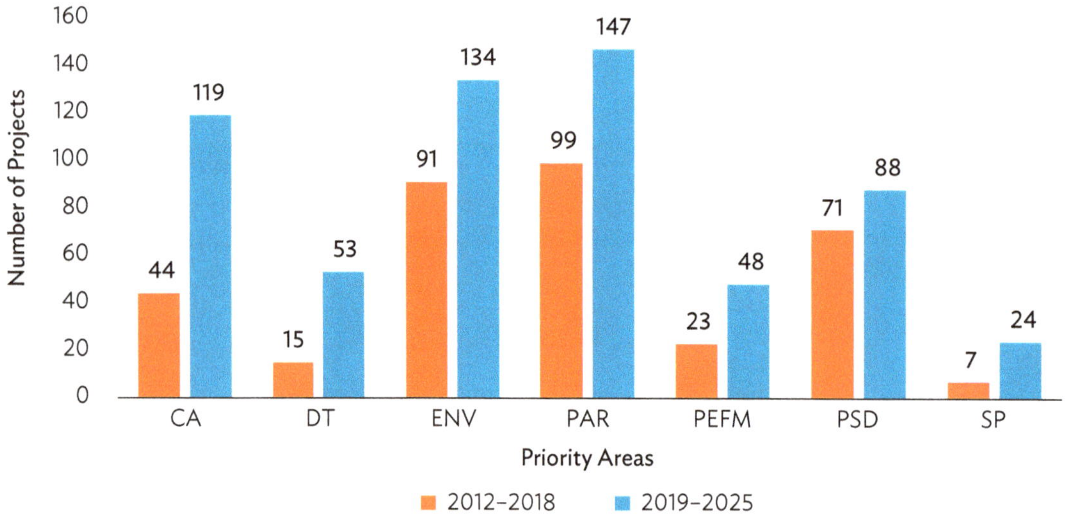

CA = climate adaptation, DT = digital technology, ENV = environmental sustainability, PAR = partnerships, PEFM = public expenditure and fiscal management, PSD = private sector development, SP = social protection.

Source: ADB.

Projects supporting priority areas have increased. Strategy 2030 identified priority areas for stepped-up support in FCAS and SIDS, including climate adaptation, connectivity and digital technology, environmental sustainability, institutional strengthening (including public expenditure and fiscal management), private sector development, and social protection and assistance. Comparing the pre- and post-Strategy 2030 periods shows a clear increase in the number of projects that include components in these key areas (Figure 3). Further, ADB increased its support for disaster risk management through scaled-up investments in preparedness, resilience, and rapid response.

On climate adaptation, the trend over the two periods is quantifiable in both volume (projects) and value (dollar) terms. The number of projects with climate adaptation components increased from 44 to 119 projects, while the value grew from $328 million to $1.6 billion.

Delivering results remains a challenge. By completion year, success rates of ADB operations in FCAS and SIDS continued to lag overall ADB results. For the most recent 3-year period (2023–2025), 48% of completed operations in FCAS were successful, while 61% were successful in SIDS. This compares to 69% for all completed ADB operations in this period. Over the longer period of 2016–2025 and looking at all completed projects in FCAS and SIDS collectively, 59% of completed operations were successful compared to 70% for all DMCs. This reflects the challenging operational contexts but also highlights the need for ADB to continue seeking ways to improve its support. Operations in the major infrastructure sectors have been most challenging. Over 2016–2025, the sectors of energy, transport, and water and other urban infrastructure services had relatively higher numbers of completed operations in FCAS and SIDS, but relatively lower success rates. Energy completed 16 projects with a 56% success rate; transport completed 22 projects with a 32% success rate; and water and other urban infrastructure services completed 12 projects with a 17% success rate (Figure 4). More detailed and disaggregated analysis of project performance beyond the current binary *successful/unsuccessful* ex post rating practice is needed. The Fragility and Engagement Division (CCFE) will develop this to better inform actions going forward.

Project readiness needs strengthening. Weak project readiness at project approval often leads to implementation challenges, cost growth, and delays, which have knock-on effects on the successful

Figure 4: Projects in FCAS and SIDS Rated Successful by Sector, 2016–2025

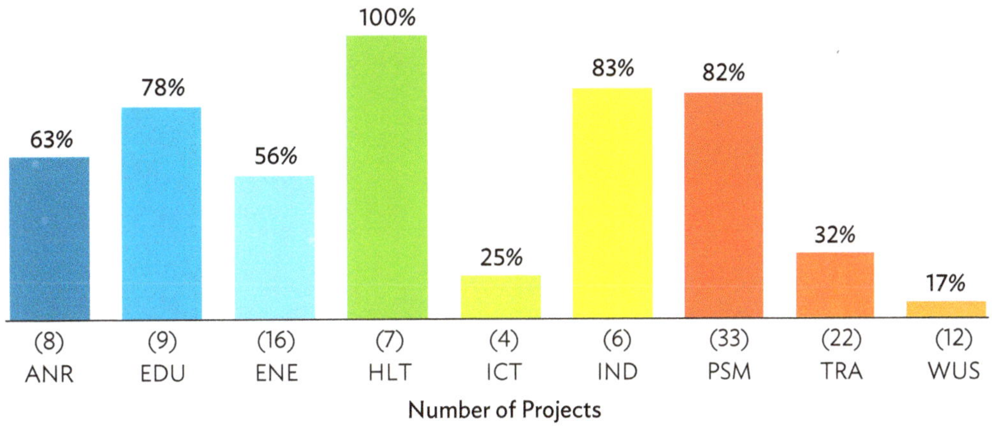

ANR = agriculture, natural resources, and rural development; EDU = education; ENE = energy; FCAS = fragile and conflict-affected situations; HLT = health; ICT = information and communication technology; IND = industry and trade; PSM = public sector management; SIDS = small island developing states; TRA = transport; WUS = water and other urban infrastructure and services.

Notes: The finance sector is excluded as only one project was completed during the period. Success rates are based on Independent Evaluation Department validation reports assessing project performance by relevance, effectiveness, efficiency, and sustainability criteria.

Source: ADB.

delivery and completion of projects. Lower success rates of completed infrastructure projects in FCAS and SIDS generally correlate with weaker project design and procurement readiness. Improving design and procurement readiness through differentiated procurement approaches is a major thrust of ongoing ADB internal training for staff working in FCAS and SIDS.[29] In addition, ADB continues to promote the use of project readiness financing to support the scale-up of sovereign and nonsovereign operations under the new capital adequacy framework; the Pacific Department has prioritized the use of project readiness financing, with currently 13 such projects ongoing and several more in the pipeline. Another area includes strengthening support during the project start-up stage, which bridges the gap between loan approval and mobilizing contractors.

On the nonsovereign side, projects in FCAS and SIDS contexts can often take longer for sponsors to develop, require higher risk-adjusted returns, and face a higher chance of not reaching financial close or achieving expected results. In private sector operations, improving design and procurement readiness is more about increased technical assistance support, including support for due diligence costs that can often be disproportionate to project costs. Stronger project readiness in FCAS and SIDS—supported by technical assistance—reduces execution risk and builds client capacity. The new methodology for monitoring readiness should help (Section IV).

Capacity constraints in DMCs continue to hinder projects. Weak capacity of DMC counterpart agencies is the most frequently cited challenge in the successful implementation of FCAS and SIDS projects, as documented in validated project completion reports and other evaluative assessments. This recurring challenge demands a more systematic and sustained approach to developing capacity in FCAS and SIDS, including at the regional level, targeting the key sector agencies with which ADB engages. This approach moves beyond the current model that typically focuses on (i) training for individual staff, (ii) shorter-term capacity development support aligned with and focused primarily on single project durations, and (iii) developing capacity mainly to ensure counterpart compliance with ADB requirements. Strengthening local capacity and leadership is not a priority, yet local actors understand the local context clearly.

[29] ADB's procurement framework provides the opportunity to differentiate procurement approaches according to country conditions.

Table 2: Success Rates of Projects Completed in 2016–2025, by Approval Years

Approval Years	Completed Projects			Ongoing Projects
	No. of Projects Rated HS/S	No. of Total Projects Rated	Success Rate	
2006–2010	15	34	44%	2
2011–2015	25	41	61%	23
2016–2020	22	32	69%	63

HS = highly successful, S = successful.

Note: The table accounts for completed projects during the period 2016–2025, grouped by approval year. Ratings are based on validations of the Independent Evaluation Department. Completed projects include regional projects and COVID-19 Pandemic Response Option (CPRO) projects. Approval periods 2001–2005 and 2021–2025 were excluded due to the small number of rated projects (eight for 2001–2005 and three for 2021–2025).

Source: ADB.

Many executing and implementing agencies face critical challenges. These relate to their core policy mandates and management functions, including planning, finance, human resources, monitoring and evaluation, operations and maintenance, and other core areas. As such, their ability to deliver on their mandates and core services—let alone support and implement externally-financed projects—is significantly hampered. More rigorous assessments of organizational mandates and performance challenges, followed by the development and implementation of long-term, flexible organizational reform and development programs, are the only effective means of transforming organizations in FCAS and SIDS contexts. Capacity assessment and support plans developed and soon to be piloted by CCFE are a first step in this direction. Stronger commitments and ownership by both ADB and DMC governments to this more comprehensive and transformational approach are needed.

Governance challenges complicate development delivery. Governance constraints are a strong determinant of weak project performance in FCAS and SIDS. Institutional drivers of fragility, such as weak rule of law, political instability, weak core public financial management functions, and fragmented public sector coordination, directly affect institutional performance and project implementation. In some countries, ministerial restructurings are frequent, as are unforeseen policy changes or reversals. These developments can undermine reform continuity or project performance. ADB needs to build resilience to institutional discontinuity and change.

The shortage of qualified consultants and contractors is a critical constraint. While this is a well-known and long-standing problem, particularly in the smaller SIDS and in countries facing unstable security conditions, it is becoming even more acute. This is driven by factors on both the demand and supply sides, including (i) the growing volume of aid-financed projects in the countries, which drives up demand and competition for good consultants and contractors; (ii) larger and more complex projects, including infrastructure projects that incorporate climate, resilience, inclusion, and other elements; (iii) steady and (in some cases) surging out-migration.

Better results from more recent projects are encouraging. While success rates by completion year of projects—the typical method for assessing performance of ADB operations—does not show any clear improvement, assessing the performance of projects by their year of approval shows a positive trend (Table 2). This trend is observed not only for FCAS and SIDS but also overall ADB operations.

Key Takeaways of Desk Review and Consultations

Findings from evaluative desk reviews and internal and external consultations are summarized below, with more details in Appendix 6.

Commitments in the FSA remain relevant, but clarification in key areas is needed. Chief among these is ADB's FCAS classification system, which relies on a national-level binary designation that fails to capture the spectrum and multidimensional nature of fragility, subnational conflicts, and cross-border spillover effects. The review also noted gaps in operational clarity around differentiated approaches for FCAS and SIDS, limitations in the usefulness of FRAs, and constraints imposed by country partnership strategy (CPS) templates that restrict deep analysis of vulnerability, resilience, and operational risk.

Stakeholders call for more transformative approaches. Feedback from consultations stressed the need to move from policy intent to practical, transformative action.[30] Stakeholders called for more tailored operational flexibilities, clearer guidance on applying diagnostics, stronger staffing and capacity measures, and incentives aligned with the higher transaction costs of working in FCAS and SIDS. Procurement, financial management, and project readiness remain overly complex, with small projects in FCAS and SIDS generally subject to the same documentation, indicators, and safeguards as large-scale operations.[31] Board members and partners emphasized the importance of addressing causes of fragility, strengthening country ownership, and sharpening ADB's value proposition through clearer priorities, results frameworks, and differentiation between FCAS and SIDS. Development partners and DMC officials encouraged deeper coordination, long-term capacity building for national institutions, and more responsive, demand-driven support. Partners also emphasized the continued relevance of the ADF for FCAS and SIDS. Stakeholders agree more ambitious, context-specific, and consistently applied approaches are essential to ADB's effectiveness and impact.

[30] Consultations were held with officials from development partners and DMCs, including Australia's Department of Foreign Affairs and Trade, Japan International Cooperation Agency, the Marshall Islands, New Zealand's Ministry of Foreign Affairs and Trade, Palau, Papua New Guinea, the World Bank, the Secretariat of the Pacific Community, and the US Office of Insular Affairs.

[31] The new Environmental and Social Framework gives flexibility to the application of safeguards requirements for low- to moderate-risk projects and should yield streamlined due diligence approaches for such projects.

IV. NEW ACTIONS TOWARD 2030

ADB's role, resources, and reputation position it well to deliver greater impact. Among many organizations supporting development, ADB is well and uniquely positioned to help DMCs address fragility, build resilience, and ensure that the most poor, vulnerable and disadvantaged groups are not left behind.[32] While ADB has remained steadfast in its support for FCAS and SIDS, its potential to be an even more relevant, responsive, and impactful partner remains strong. To meet this potential and strengthen resilience in its most fragile DMCs over the next 5 years, ADB will implement a combination of actions to enhance its engagement and results in FCAS and SIDS, supported by the three pillars of the FSA, both discussed in this chapter.

Actions to Strengthen Engagement and Results

Financing

Continue to scale-up and innovate financing. Building resilience, addressing conflicts and crises, and achieving long-term sustainable development will require continued scaling up. With additional resources available from its capital reforms, ADB is well-positioned to increase financing for FCAS and SIDS, in line with its Corporate Results Framework (CRF) target.[33] ADF has been ADB's primary financing source for FCAS and SIDS operations. Its evolution reflects the unique needs and circumstances of FCAS-classified DMCs and SIDS.[34] Meeting this

[32] External assessments of ADB reflect positively on its role as a key development partner in Asia and the Pacific, while also highlighting some areas for improvement. Recent assessments include: Multilateral Organisation Performance Assessment Network (MOPAN). 2025. *MOPAN Assessment Report: Asian Development Bank*; V. Panwar, E. Wilkinson, A. Solanki, and G. Hurley. 2026. *How Small Island Developing States View Their Development Partners: A Perceptions Survey*. Overseas Development Institute Global.

[33] The target is for 7.5% of total commitments (sovereign and nonsovereign) for FCAS and SIDS by 2030.

[34] An important feature introduced in ADF 13 (the 13th replenishment of the fund, for the 2021–2024 period) was the economic vulnerability premium, which accounts for the acute vulnerabilities of SIDS. ADF 14 continues this with an increased grant envelope and extended coverage to concessional ordinary capital resources lending allocations.

ambition will require stepped-up concessional lending, technical assistance (TA) grant resources (including fully deploying available ADF 14 resources), and nonsovereign operations. Further evolution, innovation, and application in ADB's toolkit of financing, countercyclical, and crisis-response modalities will strengthen its ability to help DMCs respond to and build resilience against the range of fragilities they face. Stepped-up mobilization of trust funds that focus on addressing FCAS and SIDS challenges should be explored. Additional financing priorities follow below.

Expand financing to address disasters, climate, and displacement. Projections show with very high certainty that (i) the frequency and severity of disasters and emergencies will continue to rise and also that long-term, slow-onset climate processes, such as sea-level rise, will continue along with their impacts, and (ii) the ability of FCAS and SIDS to manage and mitigate these will remain severely constrained, including to support the prevention of population displacement and responses to this. ADB should continue to refine existing or create new instruments and modalities, including at a regional level (e.g., Pacific program), to increase resilience, reduce disaster risk, and address disasters and emergencies. FCAS and SIDS still have limited access to pre-arranged financing despite their high vulnerability to disasters. Risk-layered financing approaches (e.g., reserve funds, contingent credit, risk transfer, and post-disaster financing) and the analytical tools required to determine optimal financing mixes for FCAS and SIDS are needed. Efforts to develop a new multi-donor trust fund should help to strengthen disaster risk financing and build capacity in disaster risk insurance in the Pacific.

With the costs of transformative adaptation and resilience-building far exceeding the financing (including borrowing) capacity of FCAS and SIDS, grant financing will become even more critical going forward, as will be new ways of financing costly but much-needed adaptation investments. Ongoing fiscal consolidation, including in some SIDS, has forced governments to make difficult trade-offs between long-term infrastructure investment, short-term repairs, and the postponement of critical projects. The next ADF replenishment will be a critical opportunity to further innovate ADB's financing for FCAS and SIDS in these areas. Ideas include mobilizing post-conflict grant financing, similar to existing mechanisms used by the World Bank and other multilateral development banks (MDBs) and regional facilities to de-risk investments and trade.

Strengthen the fragility–resilience–financing linkage. Through the ADF and other mechanisms, ADB has increasingly aligned and prioritized financing to the most vulnerable DMCs, including FCAS and SIDS. With further improvements in how ADB diagnoses fragility and resilience, ADB should be able to better target financing to specific types of fragility and risks to support prevention and resilience through new and existing financing windows or targeted projects or programs. Certain conditions can trigger eligibility for such financing. A review of how other MDBs have strengthened their fragility–resilience–financing linkages should be informative for ADB. Policy reforms to address key drivers of fragility should be part of policy dialogues in connection with policy-based loans and (in particular) policy-based grants. In addition to scaling up and innovating its financing instruments, ADB should continue support for public financial management reforms and, in particular, reforms to strengthen domestic resource mobilization.

Operations

Reform and strengthen the operational delivery model. Evidence shows that improving outcomes and results will require changes in the way ADB works with DMC clients to prepare, implement, and support projects. Diagnostics and project design, including procurement strategy, should more systematically address the key risks and challenges that often delay and derail projects or impact their longer-term sustainability and bankability (for nonsovereign operations), including structural limitations, legal and regulatory environments, political-economy dynamics, environmental and social contexts, climate exposure, and other well-documented factors. More rigorous quality-at-entry assessments can help, as can a stronger focus on strengthening project readiness. These must be packaged with recommended solutions, a support plan, and resources—so long as these processes do not add significant burden to existing processing requirements. For countries with debt distress issues, exploring the allocation of grant funds for project readiness is required. The ability to redesign programs, update outcomes and outputs, and change activities will demonstrate agility and operational relevance. Given the complex operating environments of FCAS and SIDS, robust data systems are essential for assessing intervention outcomes. Otherwise, success measures will be incomplete or unreliable. Expanding project readiness financing and closer monitoring and management of all dimensions of readiness will be critical. The new methodology for monitoring readiness should help.[35]

Further devolve and decentralize to strengthen engagement and delivery. More staff in the field will help ADB (i) engage more directly with DMC clients and partners, (ii) better understand the complex contexts and dynamics, (iii) improve the design of projects and programs, (iv) facilitate more real-time monitoring, support, and management of ongoing operations and (v) offer more opportunities to develop capacity of implementing agency staff. ADB should expand field staffing through both outposting of operational staff (sovereign, nonsovereign, sector, and thematic) and increasing resident mission-based staff. Incentives to facilitate this, especially to get high-performing staff into the most challenging contexts, should be a priority. More analysis of options and opportunities to incentivize staff, including through non-financial incentives, is needed. This may include recognition of staff who have served in FCAS or SIDS contexts as part of performance review and career progress processes. For example, the World Bank ensures recognition of an assignment in an FCAS-SIDS resident mission in subsequent assignments.

Other measures to strengthen and empower ADB offices in FCAS and SIDS should be explored, such as providing dedicated and flexible TA financing to address emerging client needs, critical evidence or data gaps, or to analyze and address complex policy, regulatory, and institutional capacity challenges. Related to this, ADB should also continue exploring new approaches to expand the availability of consultants and contractors working in FCAS and SIDS.

Strengthen enabling environments for private sector development. FCAS and SIDS have higher cost, higher risk, and more volatile investment environments, and more can be done to address critical constraints, de-risk transactions, and identify and facilitate opportunities in both new and traditional sectors. ADB's renewed focus on private sector development (PSD) as a strategic focus area (SFA), refreshed PSD shift operational approach,[36] and new CRF target for nonsovereign operations in frontier economies[37] will require that ADB takes differentiated approaches in its nonsovereign operations to a higher level in FCAS and SIDS. Actions include further strengthening the Private Sector Operations Department's field presence, tighter coordination between sovereign and nonsovereign operations (including on upstream safeguards and contextual risk assessments and diagnostics at the programming stage), closer engagement with DMCs and PSD partners, tailored processes and investment criteria for FCAS and SIDS, and creating instruments for credit enhancement. In the Pacific, continued and more focused support through teams, including the Private Sector Development Initiative, will be key. Funds for upstream and/or midstream private sector enabling programs focused on safeguards may also be useful (e.g., programs to identify and address safeguards risks per target sector or country). ADB will emphasize the areas where sovereign and nonsovereign operations can be deliberately sequenced and mutually reinforcing.[38]

35 ADB adopted a more comprehensive definition and methodology for monitoring and managing readiness in its new CRF. The five components of readiness to be tracked cover: design, financial management, institutional, procurement, and safeguards. The CRF's 2030 target for the percentage of all projects (sovereign) that are implementation-ready before approval is 75%, with a baseline (2023) of 65%. For the ADF, which includes primarily FCAS and SIDS recipients, the 2023 baseline is notably lower at 49% and there is no set target, although this will be a critical tracking indicator for ADB's operations across all sectors in FCAS and SIDS. See: ADB. 2024. *Steering ADB's Corporate Strategy to Success: Corporate Results Framework, 2025–2030*.

36 ADB. 2025. *ADB's Private Sector Development Shift Operational Approach*.

37 The target is for 50% of committed nonsovereign operations in frontier economies, which includes FCAS and SIDS.

38 In the Pacific, a coherent upstream–midstream–downstream PSD approach—using analytics to shape sovereign operations, advisory to build bankable pipelines, and nonsovereign finance to catalyze investment—while ADB Wayfinder and Frontier programs streamline processes, deploy blended finance, and back high-growth small and medium-sized enterprises, will create a resilient and self-reinforcing system that can deliver ADB's PSD ambitions.

Ensure continued alignment with SFAs and governance. ADB engagement with and support for FCAS and SIDS should continue to align with and address the SFAs of climate action, PSD, regional cooperation and public goods, digital transformation, and resilience and empowerment. ADB's support for FCAS and SIDS generally aligns with resilience and empowerment—as such, this plan is an important commitment toward strengthening this area. Other parts of this action plan address the other strategic focus areas, and Appendix 7 provides further discussion on the first four areas. A particular priority for FCAS and SIDS is governance. Governance constraints are a strong determinant of weak project performance in FCAS and SIDS. In some countries, ministerial restructurings are frequent, and new ministries are established, driven by political motivation. These undermine reform continuity or project performance. ADB needs to build resilience to institutional discontinuity and change.

Transform the approach to capacity development. ADB needs a more systematic and sustained program of support for organizational development in key sector agencies. Especially in FCAS contexts, rationalizing uncoordinated capacity building support across multiple ADB TA projects and development partner interventions based on strong anchoring in a government or academic institution, proper participant vetting, and systematic impact monitoring are all critical. Long-term support for organizational and institutional development, including at the regional level, is imperative, especially given new and complex challenges, such as high out-migration and loss of skills in some FCAS and SIDS. Given the significant disparity in living standards between Pacific FCAS–SIDS and developed economies, reversing these human capital losses may be unrealistic in the near term. How ADB uses TA to support and sustain long-term capacity development in FCAS and SIDS will be important. The new ADB TA Policy and Center of Excellence (ADBx) concept provides opportunities to support this.[39] Recent efforts by the Pacific Department to strengthen country systems through partnerships with central agencies, like public service commissions, are a good start. In de facto government contexts and smaller SIDS, capacity development support for the private sector and civil society can add value.

Support digital transformation. Digital solutions offer opportunities, such as through the use of standardized digital platforms for procurement, financial management, safeguards tracking, and reporting in FCAS and SIDS. Digital-first implementation models (modular designs, standardized templates, remote supervision tools) for small or low-risk projects may support capacity gaps. Structural constraints in FCAS and SIDS, including extreme geographical dispersion, limited human capital, and small private sectors, often impede the implementation of ADB operations. While these factors pose challenges for digital adoption, properly implemented digital solutions, supported by resilient digital foundations, sustainable governance, and institutional capacity building, can act as a catalyst to address structural barriers and transform public service delivery.

Partnerships and Coordination

Improve coordination and regional cooperation. A more congested and complex aid landscape in FCAS and SIDS demands better coordination and collaboration among key partners, especially given capacity and coordination constraints. Steps are necessary to reduce fragmentation and improve MDB architecture. The new full mutual reliance framework between ADB and the World Bank is a positive step in this direction. Greater use of joint programming and operational arrangements, more systematic use of country and regional systems, support for country-owned reforms and priorities, and stronger readiness and capacity building facilities at the country and regional levels will help develop joined-up solutions. Exploring approaches on shared digital foundations where country capacity cannot sustain multiple parallel systems is needed, as is greater attention to interoperability across partner systems (data, platforms, standards) to reduce fragmentation in FCAS and SIDS. In the Pacific, new and stronger partnership arrangements with regional organizations are needed, as well as renewed approaches to fostering regional cooperation and integration more broadly, in line with ongoing changes in the regional architecture. In the Pacific, exclusion from the global financial system and the limited availability of trade finance are challenges that lend themselves to greater regional cooperation.

[39] ADB. 2026. *Technical Assistance Policy and Establishment of ADB Center of Excellence*.

Strengthen partnerships for crisis preparedness and challenging situations. In contexts of active conflict, major disasters, de facto government situations, and other types of crisis events, ADB has supported vulnerable and impacted populations through partnerships with organizations that are better positioned and equipped to operate in these circumstances, including civil society organizations. These types of events will continue or even increase in the coming years. A regional approach to crisis preparedness and situations will continue to be crucial, particularly for Pacific countries. If ADB determines to provide support, the bank will continue to rely on the services of other organizations. Established partnerships, such as through framework agreements, support responses across these types of situations, especially in circumstances that require rapid response and support. ADB may consider framework-type arrangements or pre-qualifying organizations to be available to respond in urgent situations.

Coherence and Capabilities

Strengthen differentiated approaches with emphasis on speed and flexibility. ADB needs a bold and ambitious approach to systematically identify policies and processes that constrain the efficiency and effectiveness of its support for FCAS and SIDS. While differentiated approaches should result in more effective outcomes, speed and flexibility should remain priority considerations. All departments and offices across ADB should identify how they can do this. For example, very small SIDS projects may use simplified business processes. ADB's ability to identify and document differentiated approaches in projects should improve. Moreover, tagging projects that address some aspect of FCAS across all DMCs (not just in FCAS and SIDS) should be considered. Better tagging and reporting of differentiated approaches and attention to FCAS throughout country programming and the project cycle will provide a clearer picture of ADB's work on these priorities. This may require an upgrade of ADB's systems and templates. A more rigorous and intentional approach to streamlining the processing of sovereign operations for FCAS and SIDS is needed. These are explored as part of Pillar 1 (below).

Deepen expertise in risk, conflict, and political-economy analytics. Efforts underway by CCFE, the Economic Research and Development Impact Department, and others to strengthen country risk monitoring should continue. These will help ADB better understand the complex development dynamics and drivers of fragility that impact its DMCs. Of particular importance will be to better understand and monitor latent fragility, underlying risks that may impact stability and longer-term development progress. Furthermore, CCFE's FCAS and SIDS Unit should continue to strengthen its competencies in key knowledge areas, including fragility and resilience diagnostics, conflict analysis, crisis response, displacement, political economy-related analytics, and digital technology, with a focus on practical solutions and implementation readiness to address human resource gaps and capacity constraints. It should also strengthen its quality-at-entry support for project teams.

Actions Under the Three FSA Pillars

New actions strengthen differentiated approaches, capacity, and diagnostics. Action Plan, 2026–2030 is built on the existing three pillars, yet reflects institutional and external changes since the FSA's approval in 2021. For example, the plan leverages opportunities created by the NOM for more staff to work in FCAS and SIDS contexts and build their capacity under Pillar 2. It aligns with refinements from the MTR of Strategy 2030, emphasizing ADB's work in FCAS and SIDS contexts in the SFAs, including climate action, PSD, regional cooperation and public goods, digital transformation, and resilience and empowerment. Finally, the plan accounts for ADB's response to geopolitical disruptions since 2021, including ADB's suspension of operations in Afghanistan (footnote 17) and Myanmar (footnote 18) due to the de facto government situations in both countries. Details of Action Plan, 2026–2030 are in Appendix 2 and Appendix 3. Of the 36 actions described in the original plan, four are discrete activities already complete; the remaining 32 have been streamlined by consolidating related activities and updating their language. Eighteen actions across the three pillars comprise the new plan; they are summarized in the pillars below.

Box 3: Understanding and Addressing Fragility and Resilience

To strengthen multidimensional resilience in its developing member countries (DMCs), Asian Development Bank must continue to deepen its understanding of the dimensions and drivers of fragility and how they impact development in each context. This includes both the structural, long-term vulnerabilities and fragilities that hamper development, as well as time-bound fragilities such as crises, conflicts, and shocks that halt and/or reverse development. Among other steps outlined in Action Plan 2026–2030, the ongoing review of ADB's fragile and conflicted-affected situations classification is an opportunity to improve how ADB assesses and applies its understanding of contextual fragility and resilience across a broader spectrum of dimensions and countries and, critically, to further sharpen the focus on helping DMCs build and strengthen resilience. Although ADB has followed the multilateral development banks harmonized approach to classify fragile and conflict-affected situations in its DMCs since 2013, the other multilateral development banks participating in this approach have since designed and implemented new strategies and classification systems that more closely reflect the different challenges faced by their respective regional and country portfolios.

Source: ADB.

Redouble efforts to streamline and differentiate business processes (Pillar 1). This will focus on improving ADB's operational effectiveness in FCAS and SIDS contexts across both sovereign and nonsovereign operations, implemented through two key action areas (KAAs). Pillar 1 actions will push for more tangible changes to procurement, financial management, gender, environmental and social framework implementation, private sector operations, and monitoring. ADB will review progress under existing differentiated approaches, particularly in procurement, to propose further differentiated approaches to boost project outcomes.

Strengthen ADB capacity to work in challenging contexts (Pillar 2). Strengthening ADB's institutional capacity will be done by attracting and retaining staff with the right competencies, ensuring staff are equipped to apply differentiated approaches, enhancing access to relevant thematic knowledge and analytics, and improving monitoring and reporting of ADB-financed operations in FCAS and SIDS. These actions will include expanding the learning and development pathway for staff to work effectively in FCAS and SIDS and identifying and institutionalizing good practices. ADB will deliver relevant knowledge products on crosscutting issues such as climate security, forced displacement, conflict-sensitivity, and more, working with and through knowledge and technical partnerships that also support operations.

Sharpen diagnostics and understanding of complex contexts (Pillar 3). These actions underscore that effective differentiated approaches require a deeper understanding of DMC contexts and the drivers of vulnerability, fragility, and conflict at the regional, national, subnational, and local levels. It describes the fragility and resilience assessment (FRA), a key diagnostic to identify and analyze risk, vulnerability, fragility, and resilience, as well as other FCAS-related diagnostics ADB will employ. This pillar strengthens risk-informed strategic engagement and operational decision-making through two KAAs focused on contextual diagnostics and analysis. It includes an update to ADB's FCAS-classification exercise and details assessment tools that will provide a dynamic assessment of fragility and resilience, including in non FCAS-classified DMCs (Box 3).

V. ALIGNMENT AND IMPLEMENTATION

Alignment with ADB Priorities and Planning Directions

Alignment with SFAs and institutional priorities continues. ADB's operational priorities in FCAS and SIDS are well aligned with the SFAs, including resilience and empowerment, and the evolving planning priorities and directions of ADB. Appendix 7 provides details on the five SFAs and how they relate to priorities in and for FCAS and SIDS.

The plan supports the Pacific Approach and other directional documents. This plan both (i) reflects several issues and priorities relevant to FCAS and SIDS in the Pacific and (ii) intends to inform key issues and priorities to be articulated in the next Pacific Approach. This plan also intends to inform other relevant country partnership strategies, policies, and directional documents of relevance to FCAS and SIDS. Key findings and recommendations in the forthcoming IED evaluation on ADB support for SIDS, particularly the recommendations accepted by Management, will supplement the actions in this plan.

Implementation and Monitoring Arrangements

ADB-wide ownership and commitment will be needed. The FSA and this new action plan reflect a whole-of-ADB commitment to tailored, context-specific support to its most vulnerable DMCs. Implementation will therefore be a collective responsibility, requiring all relevant departments to work collaboratively to deliver on the priorities and actions outlined in this plan. While some of the activities under KAAs across Pillars 1 and 2 may require internal departmental consensus, others will have to be approved by Management.[40] Board approval will be

[40] Such activities include revision of staff instructions, project administration instructions, procurement guidance, financial management requirements, the development and application of incentives, changes to FCAS classification system, expanded staff learning pathways, and institutional coordination and partnership mechanisms, and similar efforts under Pillars 1 and 2.

required for activities around major financial decisions and documents.[41] CCFE will work with departments and offices across the bank to deliver these activities in line with the requirements, as detailed in the Staff Instruction on implementing ADB's policy architecture.

CCFE will continue its institutional role on FCAS and SIDS. CCFE will continue to serve as the focal point for issues related to fragility, conflict risks, and small-island vulnerability. It will support, monitor, and report on the actions outlined in this plan. Beyond this, it will continue to strengthen its ability to support ADB departments and offices in their work related to FCAS and SIDS.[42] CCFE will also continue to support country and project teams with contextual analysis as requested and support operations to strengthen performance by liaising with various departments and agreeing on differentiated approaches tailored to FCAS and SIDS. CCFE will strengthen its quality-at-entry support for project teams. ADB will enhance coordination with MDBs to strengthen effective collaboration on diagnostics processes and knowledge generation, as well as explore how such coordination may be expanded to partnerships with multilateral and bilateral partners and regional bodies. CCFE will monitor and report on the FCAS and SIDS portfolio by tracking performance, preparing annual reports, identifying risks and advising on mitigation measures, and supporting strategic corporate assessments. These include contributions to financing and institutional direction documents pertaining to FCAS and SIDS, as well as to the CRF.

CRF indicators and FSA annual reports will track progress. The Action Plan, 2026–2030 progress will be measured using action trackers and results indicators. Action trackers will monitor the fulfillment of agreed actions (tasks) under each pillar of the plan. Meanwhile, CRF indicators will report the contribution of FCAS and SIDS operations to development results and strategic focus areas, among others (Appendix 8). Both monitors will be included as part of portfolio reporting in the FSA annual reports, which CCFE will continue to publish.

41 These activities comprise identification of finance and domestic resources for climate action for FCAS-classified DMCs, e.g., the Rapid Resource Reprogramming and Deployment Option (3RDO), exploring expanded use of ADF resources, an expanded use of pre-arranged financing, the Climate Resilient Debt Clause, and programmatic approaches involving policy-based lending, leveraging the ADF Crisis Response Window for eligible countries, and development of ex ante financing instruments.

42 This could include outposting to resident missions and joining processing and administration of particularly challenging or complex FCAS-SIDS projects (e.g., when a new modality is used) as co-project team leaders or as OneADB team members.

Appendix 1

THEORY OF CHANGE AND LINKS TO CORPORATE RESULTS

Theory of change. The 2021 Fragile and Conflict-Affected Situations (FCAS) and Small Island Developing States (SIDS) Approach (FSA) is guided by a theory of change (TOC) that sets out pathways to improve the portfolio performance of the Asian Development Bank (ADB) and strengthen development outcomes in FCAS and SIDS.[1] The TOC identifies the change pathways required to achieve higher-level objectives of improved developing member countries implementation and improved ADB operations by using differentiated approaches. The TOC is organized around three mutually reinforcing pillars, supported by key assumptions that underpin successful delivery. The FSA Midterm Review confirmed the continued relevance of the TOC and change pathways but identified new areas for emphasis to align with ADB's new operating model.[2] These include a strengthened focus on risk-based approaches, stronger private sector engagement, and climate change.

Causal logic. By increasing the use of differentiated approaches in FCAS and SIDS, ADB is expected to have improved business processes (Pillar 1 – such as through tailored procurement processes, contextual safeguards applications, and performance targets), stronger staff capacity and institutional arrangements (Pillar 2 – such as through increasing the number of staff outposted to FCAS and SIDS, offering staff training on working in FCAS and SIDS contexts, providing incentive structures to attract and retain staff working in these more challenging areas, and developing and disseminating knowledge specific to FCAS and SIDS), and deeper contextual understanding of DMCs (Pillar 3 – such as preparing in depth fragility and resilience assessments, drafting quick and updated watching briefs, developing a country risk monitor, and establishing the dynamic FCAS classification system). These improvements will lead to improved performance of ADB operations and DMC outcomes, which in turn will contribute to improved livelihoods, more inclusive and resilient development outcomes, and the advancement of sustainable development. Figure A1.1 illustrates their relationships.

Pillar 1: Improving responsiveness of ADB processes. This pillar focuses on adapting ADB's processes, procedures, and modalities to FCAS and SIDS needs, contexts, and risks. Activities include making project design and processing more flexible, streamlining procedures, using private sector and funding modalities, and incorporating fragility-sensitive monitoring and evaluation. The pathway strengthens the responsiveness of ADB operations aligned with DMC contexts and will improve portfolio performance.

Pillar 2: Increasing institutional capacity. The second pillar enhances ADB's ability to deliver operations in FCAS and SIDS by strengthening institutional coordination, expanding staff availability and competencies, and ensuring talent retention. Key activities include development and application of incentives, expanded staff learning pathways, and institutional coordination and partnership mechanisms. The pillar reinforces ADB's field presence through the recruitment of technical expertise to resident missions.

Pillar 3: Enhancing contextual understanding. The last pillar improves ADB's capacity to understand and respond to drivers of fragility and resilience through the strengthening of contextual knowledge and analysis and

---

[1] ADB. 2021. *Fragile and Conflict-Affected Situations and Small Island Developing States Approach*.

[2] ADB. 2024. *Summary of Midterm Review: Fragile and Conflict-Affected Situations and Small Island Developing States Approach*.

Figure A1.1: FCAS and SIDS Approach Theory of Change

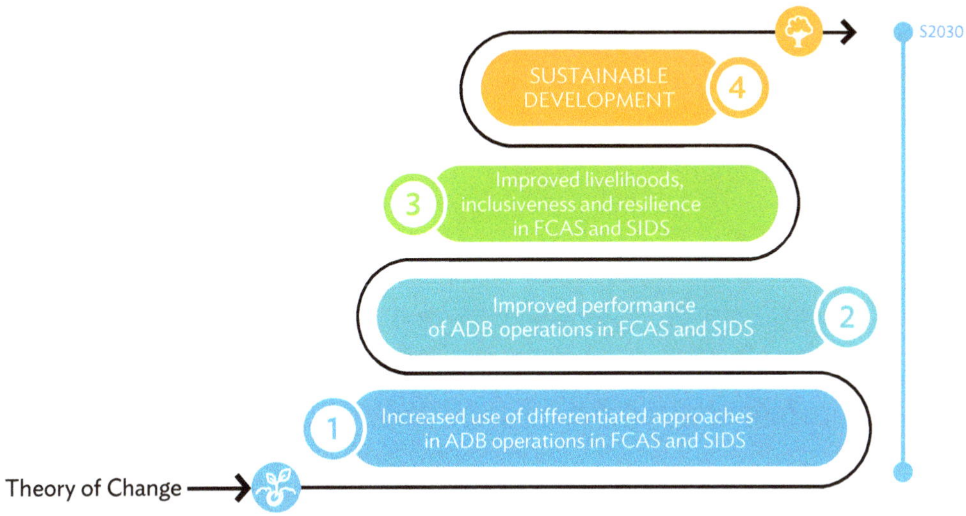

ADB = Asian Development Bank, FCAS = fragile and conflicted-affected situations, SIDS = small island developing states, S2030 = Strategy 2030.

Source: ADB.

subsequent application of the assessments to strategic engagement and operations. This pillar is about ensuring that contextual knowledge and analysis inform project design through a systematic use of multidimensional diagnostic findings.

Assumptions. Several critical assumptions underpin the TOC: (i) funds for fragility and resilience assessments are available across national, regional, local, and sector levels (A1); (ii) agreed reforms to processes and procedures are adopted and implemented (A2); (iii) the private sector accepts higher levels of risk in FCAS and SIDS (A3); and (iv) departments integrate the FSA into their operations (A4). Additional assumptions cover continuity of FCAS and SIDS Unit functions (A5), the effectiveness of the OneADB approach in FCAS and SIDS operations (A6), retention of expertise by regional departments (A7), effective engagement with DMCs and stakeholders (A8), and identification of contextual drivers of fragility and resilience during the project cycle (A9). The FSA's MTR introduced new assumptions: (a) the new operating model (NOM) private sector development shift is implemented (A3.1); (b) under the NOM, the OneADB approach is operational (A6.1); (c) NOM staff assignments are effective (A7.1); and (d) the NOM and climate shift, in line with ADB's Climate Change Action Plan, are implemented (A9.1). Collectively, these assumptions provide the conditions necessary for the TOC to be effective.

Links to Corporate Results Framework. The results framework of the FSA is rooted in the principles of the Corporate Results Framework (CRF), 2025–2030. FSA Level 1 indicators are development results indicators of the CRF but disaggregated for FCAS-classified DMCs and SIDS (1.A to 1.G). Level 2 indicators are based on CRF indicators for ADB's strategic focus areas (2.A to 2.E). Indicators measuring the success rates of completed sovereign and nonsovereign operations likewise originate from the CRF (2.F to 2.G). Lastly, Level 3 indicators, which measure the performance of ongoing projects as well as human resources, come from CRF indicators for operational management and organizational effectiveness (3.A to 3.D).

Appendix 2

PLANNED ACTIONS UNDER THREE PILLARS, 2026–2030

The three pillars of Action Plan, 2026–2030 and their respective key action areas (KAAs) and actions follow. As with any action plan, during implementation the Asian Development Bank (ADB) may adjust and refine the actions as circumstances evolve.

Pillar 1: Improving Responsiveness of Standard ADB Processes and Procedures for FCAS and SIDS Differentiated Approaches

Pillar 1 includes revising current business processes and procedures and/or developing new ones to improve operational effectiveness in fragile and conflict-affected situations (FCAS) and small island developing states (SIDS) contexts across sovereign and nonsovereign operations. These improvements will be achieved through actions in two KAAs.

KAA 1.1: New flexible business processes for sovereign operations in FCAS–SIDS applied

New flexible business processes for sovereign operations in FCAS and SIDS developed. ADB will revise its business processes for project processing, implementation, and evaluation to better suit FCAS and SIDS contexts. This includes reviewing staff instructions, project administration instructions, procurement guidance, and financial management requirements for FCAS and SIDS contexts. ADB will review differentiated approaches that other multilateral development banks (MDBs) apply in FCAS and SIDS contexts and contribute to MDB working groups on such topics. Findings from the Strategy, Policy, and Partnerships Department's sovereign business process review, which looks at the sovereign processing cycle, will be part of the proposed changes. Other areas where ADB may differentiate its business processes include environmental and social framework risk management, climate change and disaster risk management, and gender, poverty, and social dimensions. ADB will explore how to create flexibility to change outcomes, outputs, activities, and targets in FCAS-SIDS operations, where necessary. This also includes developing and applying differentiated performance targets. In addition to processes, this action includes toolkits such as the forthcoming Crisis Response Toolkit, as well as the identification of innovative finance and domestic resources for climate action for FCAS-classified developing member countries, which require more targeted support and funding options, such as the Rapid Resource Reprogramming and Deployment Option, alongside continual efforts to strengthen disaster risk management capacity and reduce residual risk.

New flexible business processes for sovereign operations in FCAS and SIDS applied. ADB will boost the use of products and modalities that support better project outcomes in FCAS and SIDS, including project readiness financing and small expenditure financing facilities for infrastructure projects. In SIDS, this may also involve an expanded use of pre-arranged financing, including ex ante financing for disasters and emergencies, the Climate Resilient Debt Clause, and programmatic approaches involving policy-based lending for public sector reforms. ADB will leverage the Asian Development Fund Crisis Response Window for eligible countries to incentivize development of ex ante financing instruments and arrangements, such as catastrophe bonds, disaster relief bonds, insurance, and regional risk pool arrangements.

KAA 1.2: New flexible business processes for nonsovereign operations in FCAS–SIDS applied

The need for flexibility in business processes for nonsovereign operations in FCAS and SIDS reviewed and addressed. This action includes processes that increase uptake of private sector investments, especially small nonsovereign transactions in FCAS and SIDS. ADB will explore business processes that increase its risk-bearing capacity for nonsovereign operations in FCAS and SIDS.

Innovative approaches to increase nonsovereign operations in FCAS and SIDS applied. This involves the deployment of new approaches, programs, or modalities that will enable and increase nonsovereign operations in FCAS and SIDS and increasing the use of technical assistance on a non-reimbursable basis to originate and monitor debt and equity transactions in FCAS and SIDS. Differentiated and innovative approaches need to be applied beyond transaction processing to have an impact on measurement and monitoring. Approaches should recognize that the relative size of transactions to market has a direct relationship to the likely additionality of the transaction to the wider market impact. Market context shapes additionality, with stronger impact in FCAS and SIDS contexts. By developing new, innovative internal approaches to guarantee ADB's portfolio of debt in FCAS and SIDS DMCs, ADB can pursue development impact while reducing the risk of capital losses.

Pillar 2: Increasing ADB's Institutional Capacity for Operations in FCAS and SIDS

Increasing ADB's institutional capacity for operations in FCAS and SIDS at both the strategic and operational levels requires attracting and retaining staff with the right competencies to work in FCAS and SIDS contexts. These staff need the right skills to apply differentiated approaches. Actions in four KAAs support this pillar.

KAA 2.1: Organizational support to FCAS and SIDS augmented

Further build the pool of staff with competencies to work in FCAS-SIDS contexts. Recruiting and transferring competent and motivated staff, increasing outposting opportunities and short-term assignments between FCAS and SIDS contexts and headquarters (both directions), and expanding the allocation of positions based in FCAS and SIDS through the annual work program and budget framework exercise, which prioritizes positions in FCAS and SIDS under the Pacific Approach, will deepen ADB's talent pool.

Apply enhanced incentive structures to attract and retain staff to work in FCAS and SIDS. Effective financial and nonfinancial incentive structures to attract high-capacity staff to work in FCAS and SIDS contexts include hardship location provisions, job security following field assignments, and benefit adjustments to fill gaps in service availability—such as health care—in different resident missions. Simultaneously, rethinking incentive mechanisms can attract staff who are motivated to achieving meaningful results in highly challenging contexts. Incentives information can be communicated and readily available to all staff.

KAA 2.2: ADB staff application of differentiated approaches in FCAS and SIDS enhanced

Expand the learning and development pathway for staff to work effectively in FCAS and SIDS. ADB will ensure staff in FCAS- and SIDS-related roles have suitable knowledge resources and support by expanding learning opportunities, including training modules and resources. Staff will have an increased strategic and operational understanding of differentiated approaches and how to apply contextual knowledge about FCAS and SIDS (e.g., tools for understanding country context, supporting capacity development, applying conflict sensitive, do-no-harm approaches). Fit-for-purpose learning and development options will be provided for new, and FCAS and SIDS-experienced staff, including country directors and managers assuming posts in FCAS-SIDS contexts. The learning and development pathway will include international and national staff supporting both sovereign and nonsovereign operations.

Strengthen the FCAS and SIDS peer learning network as a community of practice. The FCAS and SIDS peer learning network will be strengthened and operate as a community of practice. It will facilitate informal discussions and sharing of good practices, while also offering a professional network for staff working in

FCAS and SIDS. It will support the institutionalization and expansion of good practice, which may be initiated on an individual basis to support the "regularizing" of differentiated approaches.

KAA 2.3: Thematic knowledge and analytics on FCAS–SIDS produced and disseminated

Continue to deliver relevant knowledge and analytical work to support staff in FCAS and SIDS. ADB will develop high-impact and demand-driven data analytics, knowledge products and services, and tools that will directly support ADB operations and the evolution of ADB's FCAS and SIDS agenda. Focus areas will be informed by broader global risks and development trends which have regional and local impact on vulnerability, fragility, and resilience in FCAS and SIDS contexts. Tailored knowledge products will enhance operations by providing a nuanced understanding of implications in FCAS and SIDS DMCs, identifying evidence for building resilience in FCAS and SIDS contexts. The knowledge agenda will work across sectors and departments and include issues such as economic migration and forced displacement, capacity development, climate security, private sector development, critical minerals, conflict sensitivity, and peace and development, all in the context of FCAS and SIDS.

Explore new knowledge and technical partnerships for more effective work in FCAS and SIDS contexts at the headquarters and country level. ADB will strategically expand and/or deepen existing global, regional, and country-specific partnerships and engagement in knowledge-sharing, capacity-strengthening, and joint assessment and analytical work in DMCs. It also includes increasing coordination at the country level with development partners on joint programming and funding, as well as collaborating in global fora, such as with multilateral development bank working groups and platforms, and with international agencies and organizations focused on fragility, conflict, and violence, and broader FCAS- and SIDS-related topics, which will enhance knowledge and also support operational partnerships. ADB will continue to be an active member of the Multilateral Development Bank Coordination Platform on economic migration and forced displacement, as well as the convener of the cross-departmental working group within ADB.

Update and implement an outreach strategy to communicate findings of knowledge products, evaluations, and analytics to relevant stakeholders. A communications and engagement strategy, updated annually, will promote and facilitate effective knowledge management and transfer of FCAS and SIDS differentiated approaches, knowledge products, and analytics. The use of ADB's institutional artificial intelligence tools and knowledge management systems will also be deployed.

KAA 2.4: FCAS and SIDS portfolio monitoring and FSA reporting operational

Ensure the dedicated dashboard and monitoring tools for ADB's FCAS-SIDS portfolio align with SovOps developments. ADB will maintain a dedicated dashboard and tools to monitor the FCAS and SIDS portfolio and the progress of key performance indicators, including the FSA results indicators and the actions of Action Plan, 2026–2030.

Prepare and disseminate annual reports on FSA implementation to monitor and guide ADB on FSA delivery. The FSA report will provide ADB Management with an annual status of the FSA's implementation, including across the strategic focus areas (SFAs). A midterm review in 2028 and an evaluation at the end of the FSA in 2030 are planned, which will enable reflection on ADB's progress in successfully applying differentiated approaches and allow for any needed course correction.

Pillar 3: Enhancing Understanding of DMC Contexts

Implementing differentiated approaches for successful development outcomes in FCAS and SIDS requires detailed contextual understanding of DMCs and the drivers and dynamics of increasing vulnerability, fragility, and conflict at the regional, national, subnational, and local levels. Pillar 3 enhances effective, risk-informed ADB strategic engagement and operational approaches through a robust understanding of specific DMC contexts. This will be achieved through actions in two KAAs:

KAA 3.1: Contextual knowledge and analysis of DMCs strengthened

Prepare multidimensional diagnostics including fragility and resilience assessments (FRAs), political economy analyses, watching briefs, and related risk assessment work for ADB Management and staff. FRAs are diagnostic tools that (i) identify and analyze risk, vulnerability, fragility, and resilience at the country or project level and (ii) consider the implications of fragility and resilience for ADB strategic engagement and operations, including project design and preparation. Additional FCAS-related diagnostics, such as political economy analyses and watching briefs, will inform operations and support country programming teams. Such analysis can help lay out why capacities remain weak (low public service remuneration, high turnover, political interference) and identify which institutional reforms are foundational in country-specific contexts. Short-version briefings and presentations of key FCAS findings will also help ensure provision of timely and relevant information on DMC risk profiles to ADB Management and staff. Diagnostics and knowledge work must directly address FCAS and SIDS priorities, based on robust analysis of country circumstances, and clearly linked to the development of both sovereign and nonsovereign project pipelines. Sector assessments, country diagnostic studies, and knowledge products should systematically address country constraints and feed into pipeline formulation and project design or policy changes. Diagnostics could also systematically assess digital readiness and digital risks (connectivity, interoperability, data protection, cybersecurity) as part of FRAs where relevant.

Strengthen systematic and regular monitoring of vulnerability, fragility, and resilience dimensions of FCAS and at-risk DMCs, including SIDS, for improved understanding of potential contextual challenge and disruption. ADB will develop a country risk monitor to track fragility and conflict indicators across all DMCs on potentially disruptive situations (including but not limited to debt distress, climate fragility, political and economic crises, mass protests and/or civil unrest, forced displacement, insurgency and armed conflict, and spillover effects) at the regional, national, and subnational levels. Identified trends and movement will help (i) signal advance warning of disruption and (ii) gauge acute and chronic risks across the political, societal, economic, institutional, structural, and environmental spectrum of ADB's fragility and resilience framework.

Revise and implement ADB's FCAS classification system and assessment tools. The revised classification system will address gaps in the existing classification system in the multidimensional nature and manifestation of fragility and resilience, including capturing cross-border regional effects into non-FCAS classified countries. It will incorporate a cohesive spectrum of specifically calibrated indicators that enable rigorous, systematic, and dynamic assessment of all DMCs for FCAS. It will not only improve country identification but will also inform risk analysis and identify areas for targeted support. Moreover, the revised classification system envisages enabling ADB to (i) trigger financial eligibility through dedicated funding mechanisms; (ii) activate operational flexibilities in project preparation, procurement, and implementation; and (iii) support and inform advanced monitoring and evaluation, Environmental and Social Framework application, and country portfolio monitoring. ADB will undertake to identify and learn from what other MDBs have done to provide specific funding based on fragility classifications.

KAA 3.2 Multidimensional FCAS diagnostic assessments applied to strategic engagement and operations

Strengthen the strategic application and operational linkages of fragility and resilience assessments and tools, in collaboration with a wide range of stakeholders and highlighting ADB's five SFAs. The value of FCAS diagnostic tools is realized when their findings and recommendations are integrated in country partnership strategies, and project design and implementation. Expanding interdepartmental working relationships and linkages, including with resident and regional missions, will enable ADB to more consistently apply relevant knowledge—including deeper analysis in its SFAs—in country partnership strategy preparation and programming, and investment pipeline formulation. Findings and resilience actions of project-level diagnostics will be more systematically integrated into project design and preparation, using tailored FCAS knowledge products for project teams. ADB will continue to broaden its base of external stakeholders for preparation of FCAS diagnostics, including development partners, civil society organizations, nonstate organizations, and minority groups.

Explore quality-at-entry support for new operations in FCAS and SIDS contexts. ADB will design and apply an expanded and consistent conflict and fragility lens to project preparation in FCAS and SIDS contexts, ultimately mainstreaming this analysis into business processes as described under Pillar 1, to inform and adapt project design as appropriate, including the underlying design and monitoring framework. This will ensure that outcomes and outputs of FCAS and SIDS projects are feasible, while strengthening project monitoring through indicators that are measurable and for which data sources exist. The FCAS and SIDS Unit will provide advisory support for new operations through expanded collaboration with sector departments and active participation in country management and project teams. This will ensure findings and recommendations of FCAS diagnostic assessments and tools are applied during project preparation and administration.

Appendix 3

PLANNED PILLAR 1 AND PILLAR 2 DETAILED ACTIONS

Table A3.1: List of Business Processes for Review

	Planned Action	Responsible Division	Expected Date
1	Conduct a review and assessment of ADB's procurement processes for FCAS and SIDS that considers issues such as timelines and capacity requirements. Review and update the *FCAS, SIDS, and Emergency Situations: Guidance Note on Procurement* and reflect corresponding updates in the Staff Instruction on procurement.	PPFD, CCFE	2026–27
2	Provide dedicated content on adb.org for procurement in FCAS and SIDS with knowledge products, links, events, and case studies.	PPFD, CCFE	2026 onwards
3	Develop dedicated FCAS and SIDS procurement templates, engaging with other development partners where feasible.	PPFD	2026 onwards
4	Apply bid-securing declarations by default for nationally advertised procurement.	PPFD	2026 onwards
5	Explore the feasibility of establishing a pool of regional consultants from Pacific DMCs, between national and international levels.	PPFD	2026 onwards
6	Conduct local bidding clinics prior to advertisement of nationally advertised packages on projects.	PPFD	2026 onwards
7	Identify opportunities for targeted aggregation of commonly procured items such as emergency response supplies, vehicles, IT equipment, etc.	PPFD	2026 onwards
8	Explore options to conduct due diligence in advance for entities that are willing to work with ADB in conflict contexts like Afghanistan[1] and Myanmar[2] to enable them to be mobilized quickly if needed.	PPFD, CCFE	2026 onwards
9	Update the *FCAS, SIDS, and Emergency Situations: Technical Guidance Note on Financial Management* and reflect updates in the Staff Instruction on financial management.	PFFM	2027
	(i) Allocate more TA and staff resources to support financial management delivery and performance.	PFFM	2026 onwards

continued on next page

[1] ADB placed its regular assistance to Afghanistan on hold effective 15 August 2021, with ADB providing support for basic human needs through United Nations agencies.

[2] ADB's regular assistance to Myanmar has been on hold since 1 February 2021, with ADB providing support for basic human needs through United Nations agencies.

Table A3.1 *continued*

	Planned Action	Responsible Division	Expected Date
	(ii) Expand training and capacity building for financial management to executing and implementing agencies and supreme audit institutions. Conduct project-specific training and/or clinics to further develop capacity. Support supreme audit institution capacity and system strengthening.	PFFM	2026 onwards
	(iii) Implement country-level financial management action plans through a range of supportive actions.	PFFM	2026 onwards
10	Develop advice on the operations and maintenance of projects for sustainability in FCAS and SIDS contexts. Explore the possibility of dedicated loans and/or TA supporting long-term operations and the maintenance of assets financed under ADB projects.	SPD, CCFE, Regional and Sectors departments	2027
11	Develop a good practice note on preparing a design and monitoring framework in FCAS and SIDS contexts.	CCFE, SPD, PPFD	2026
12	Develop guidance for ADB on promoting gender equality in FCAS and SIDS contexts.	CCFE, CCGE	2026
13	Enhance tools for capacity development and measurement, guiding ADB's institutional support through needs assessment and evidence of effectiveness, based on an assessment of need and evidence of what works.	CCFE	2026–27
14	To address capacity constraints, explore accord arrangements with entities such as United Nations Volunteers, Australian Volunteers Program, and Japan International Cooperation Agency's volunteer program to either directly engage volunteers for projects when ADB has been delegated procurement of consultants, or enable single sourcing when there is no delegation of procurement to ADB.	Regional and Sectors departments	Ongoing
15	Prepare guidance to strengthen project rationales when supporting the Resilience and Empowerment strategic focus area.	SPD, CCFE	2027
16	Update ADB guidance on working with de facto governments.	OGC, Afghanistan and Myanmar Resident Missions	2026
17	Update approach papers for Afghanistan and Myanmar.	multiple	From 2026
18	Provide support to apply the Environmental and Social Framework in FCAS-SIDS contexts. Assess the tools, methods, and procedures necessary to implement the framework for their applicability to FCAS-SIDS and propose alternatives for those that cannot be effectively implemented in FCAS-SIDS.	OSFG	2026
19	Strengthen country safeguard systems by working with development partners (e.g., World Bank, Australia) to (i) provide long-term support to key agencies to improve social and environmental management, (ii) conduct safeguard assessments in selected FCAS–SIDS, and (iii) reduce transaction costs through the Full Mutual Reliance Framework and/or the Pacific Region Infrastructure Facility Shared Approach for safeguard implementation. Work with regional partners (e.g., Secretariat of the Pacific Regional Environmental Programme) to develop and implement an action plan that coordinates strengthening of country safeguard systems.	OSFG	Ongoing

continued on next page

Table A3.1 *continued*

	Planned Action	Responsible Division	Expected Date
20	Develop and implement training for contractors on how to design and implement contractor environmental and social management plans. Train consultants (national and international) on how to design and implement environmental and social assessment in FCAS–SIDS.	OSFG	Ongoing
21	Assess the proposed private sector portfolio in FCAS–SIDS to identify opportunities to systematically reduce environmental and social risks to increase the private sector downstream portfolio.	OSFG, PSOD	2026
22	Develop an Environmental and Social Safeguards framework for cost recovery for nonsovereign operations TA transactions which support small and medium-size enterprises operating in FCAS and SIDS.	OSFG, PSOD	Ongoing
23	Launch a multi-donor SIDS Disaster Risk Mitigation Finance Facility.	CCDR	2026
24	Leverage the ADF Crisis Response Window for eligible countries to incentivize development of ex ante financing instruments and arrangements, such as catastrophe bonds, disaster relief bonds, insurance, and regional risk pool arrangements.	CCDR	Ongoing
25	Finalize the Crisis Response Toolkit.	SPD, CCDR	2026

ADB = Asian Development Bank; ADF = Asian Development Fund; CCFE = Fragility and Engagement Division; CCGE = Gender Equality Division; CCDR = Disaster Risk Management Division; FCAS = fragile and conflict-affected situation; OGC = Office of the General Counsel; OSFG = Office of Safeguards; PPFD = Procurement, Portfolio, and Financial Management Department; PFFM = Financial Management Division; PSOD = Private Sector Operations Department; SIDS = small island developing states; SPD = Strategy, Policy, and Partnerships Department; TA = technical assistance.

Table A3.2: List of Planned Actions to Build ADB's Talent Pool of Staff

	Planned Action	Responsible Division	Expected Date
1	Conduct a trend analysis on applicants and ADB staff outposted and working in FCAS–SIDS. To support increased uptake of outposting and short-term assignments, identify applicant demographics to understand if there are patterns or barriers for some groups.	BPCT	2026
2	Review the financial support and incentives for staff posted in FCAS–SIDS and similar contexts through the 2026 CBR.	BPRS	2026
3	Communicate and make readily available information to staff about working in FCAS-SIDS field offices (e.g., outposting fairs, AskHR articles, Field Office Benefits Calculator, Q&A with staff in-country), including financial and non-financial benefits. For example, detail hardship location provisions that ADB provides (danger allowances, rest and recuperation breaks), and how the CBR provides support to staff in FCAS–SIDS and similar field offices.	BPCT, BPRS	2026 onwards
4	Develop regional officer staff positions for sector and thematic areas in FCAS–SIDS where the needed skills and/or experience cannot be found and/or when a supervisor will not be co-located in the country. The support for these positions in terms of benefits will be assessed as part of the 2026 CBR, which is assessing support to hardship locations.	BPRS	2026

continued on next page

Table A3.2 *continued*

	Planned Action	Responsible Division	Expected Date
5	Strengthen ADB oversight of project implementation through expanded outposting to resident missions of international sector experts as well as procurement and financial management staff to ensure that elevated fiduciary risks are managed appropriately.	Sectors Department, PPFD, BPMSD	Ongoing
6	Support learning and development of staff assigned to FCAS–SIDS through both CCFE-led training and fragility and resilience modules integrated into other training programs.	CCFE, BPOD-LDU	Ongoing
7	Support staff working in FCAS and SIDS with digital skills, such as on digital public infrastructure (payments, registries, data exchange), cybersecurity and data governance, and the use of digital tools for supervision, remote monitoring, and analytics.	DIG	Ongoing
8	Provide tailored resources for self-directed learning and development for staff posted to FCAS–SIDS.	CCFE, BPOD-LDU	Ongoing
9	Strengthen capacity of managers (country directors and regional directors) who will be posted to FCAS-SIDS contexts, with tailored coaching, context training, and peer learning.	CCFE, BPOD-LDU	Ongoing
10	Convene sector department and regional department staff who cover FCAS-SIDS contexts to facilitate learning through a strengthened peer learning network community of practice.	CCFE	Ongoing
11	Review and discuss staffing requirements through the annual WPBF process to assess demands in a holistic manner and align with ADB strategic priorities, including for FCAS and SIDS.	BPOD-SWU	Annual
12	Strengthen capacity of CCFE. Continue to strengthen its competencies in key knowledge areas, including fragility and resilience diagnostics, conflict analysis, crisis response, displacement, political economy-related analytics, and digital technology, with a focus on practical solutions and implementation readiness to address human resource gaps and capacity constraints. Build its quality-at-entry support for project teams.	CCFE, BPMSD	Ongoing

ADB = Asian Development Bank; BPCT = Culture and Talent Division; BPMSD = Budget, Personnel, and Management Systems Department; BPOD = Budget and People Operations Division; BPRS = Reward, HR, and Health Services Division; CBR = Comprehensive Benefits Review; CCFE = Fragility and Engagement Division; DIG = Digital Sector Office; FCAS = fragile and conflict-affected situations; LDU = Learning and Development Unit; PPFD = Procurement, Portfolio, and Financial Management Department; SIDS = small island developing states; SWU = Strategic Workforce Unit; WPBF = Work Program and Budget Framework.

Appendix 4

MULTILATERAL DEVELOPMENT BANKS' FRAGILITY AND CONFLICT STRATEGIES

AFRICAN DEVELOPMENT BANK (2022)

Strategy Document: Strategy for Addressing Fragility and Building Resilience in Africa (2022–2026)

Focus. The strategy aims to strengthen the engagement of the African Development Bank (AfDB) on fragility by shifting to a preventative approach that addresses root causes of conflict and builds resilience against shocks. Recognizing fragility can occur in any context, it emphasizes scaling up crisis prevention and adapting operations to diverse vulnerabilities across Africa.

Diagnostic Tool. The **Country Resilience and Fragility Assessment** evaluates fragility through six criteria: political inclusiveness, safety and security, justice, social cohesion, regional contagion, and climate change.

Funding. AfDB's **Transition Support Facility** provides concessional financing to countries affected by fragility and conflict, leveraging over $6.7 billion in additional development finance.

Approach. The strategy adopts flexible, context-specific interventions across four situations on the fragility spectrum:

- Rising risks of conflict or state collapse
- Active conflict or prolonged crisis
- Post-crisis recovery and reform
- Reduced risks and pathways to resilience

It refines AfDB's 2014 definition of fragility and updates it to be:
"A condition where exposure to internal or external pressures exceeds existing capacities to prevent, respond to, and recover from them, creating risks of instability."

Guiding Principles

- **Prevention** – Use fragility assessments to anticipate risks and build resilience.
- **Selectivity** – Prioritize operations with the greatest resilience impact.
- **Patience** – Maintain long-term engagement through instability.
- **Do No Harm** – Apply conflict-sensitive, gender-responsive safeguards.
- **Ownership** – Engage governments, civil society, and local actors early.
- **Partnerships** – Coordinate with development, humanitarian, and peacebuilding actors.

Operational Levers

- Systematic application of a fragility lens in planning and project design
- Expanded analytical work and results management
- Increased staff presence and tailored capacity building in fragile contexts
- Scaled-up investments using fit-for-purpose instruments and mobilizing additional finance
- Outreach and communication to strengthen partnerships and resource mobilization

Strategic Priorities

- **Institutional capacity** – Build effective national and regional institutions, focusing on economic and financial governance.
- **Resilient societies** – Invest in infrastructure and services to reduce isolation, address gender inequalities, promote economic diversification, and improve access to basic services.
- **Private Investment** – Foster conditions for private sector growth and job creation, especially for women and youth, through direct investments, support for financial institutions, and de-risking instruments to attract domestic and foreign capital.

DEVELOPMENT BANK OF LATIN AMERICA AND THE CARIBBEAN (2025)

Strategy Document: Strategic Framework for Security and Justice for Development

Focus. The framework focuses on the interdependency between security and sustainable and inclusive development in Latin America and the Caribbean, acknowledging the relationship between violence, inequality, low productivity, and reduced economic growth. The framework outlines how the Development Bank of Latin America and the Caribbean (CAF) will confront organized crime to reduce violence and corruption through a strategic and operational approach to the security and justice sector. CAF's support focuses on (i) information and evidence to support policy advice and security policy development, and (ii) execution and governance to strengthen institutions, including coordination, capacity building, and the provision of tools.

Principles

- Multidimensional, recognizing the complex and multifaceted nature of insecurity and crime and moving beyond traditional security approaches to center on citizens.
- Multilevel, aiming to foster collaboration between local, national, and transnational governments.
- Networked action, to ensure coordinated efforts among the state, civil society, private sector, and academia.

Key features of the approach

The framework is a sector roadmap that outlines a support approach on security and justice for CAF member countries. It focuses on prevention and protection; policing and criminal investigation; the justice system; the prison system; and support and rehabilitation.

EUROPEAN INVESTMENT BANK (2022)

Strategy Document: EIB Strategic Approach to Fragility and Conflict

Focus. The approach of the European Investment Bank (EIB) aims to make its engagement in fragile and conflict-affected situations more coherent, efficient, and impactful. It seeks to strengthen operational and institutional capabilities to act swiftly during crises while aligning with European Union (EU) external action goals on conflict prevention, peace, and stability.

Tools. The bank leverages EU-wide instruments such as **Country-Level Conflict Analysis Screening** and **Multi-Annual Indicative Programme reviews** to inform its interventions.

Funding. No dedicated financing vehicle exists; however, EIB channels innovative, high-impact financing into fragile and conflict-affected contexts through its existing funds.

Approach. The approach influences all aspects of EIB operations, focusing on:

- Enhancing support for impact-driven projects
- Improving sustainability and resilience of investments
- Strengthening project origination and impact measurement
- Promoting institutional learning on fragility and conflict
- Increasing visibility of EIB's work in these contexts

Principles

- **Policy first** – Full alignment with EU policies and coherence across institutions.
- **Contextualization** – Deep understanding of local drivers of fragility to design tailored responses.
- **Impact-driven investment** – Prioritize projects that prevent conflict, strengthen resilience, and support recovery.
- **Conflict sensitivity** – Ensure "do no harm" and, where possible, contribute to peacebuilding efforts.
- **Social sustainability and inclusion** – Address exclusion and inequality as root causes of fragility, guided by EIB's Social Sustainability Framework.

Key Features

- **Peace-positivity** – Move beyond conflict sensitivity to actively address fragility drivers.
- **Engagement orientations** – Four guiding directions for different fragility contexts.
- **Conflict sensitivity helpdesk** – On-demand support for staff to assess risks and adapt project design.

Implementation Pillars

- **Operational responsiveness** – Enhance diagnostics, analytics, advisory services, and technical support to clients.
- **Institutional environment** – Strengthen local presence, build staff capacity, improve monitoring and learning, and enhance communication.
- **Strategic partnerships** – Deepen collaboration with international actors, member states, and civil society, while integrating United Nations-led agendas such as **Youth, Peace, and Security** and **Women, Peace, and Security.**

INTER-AMERICAN DEVELOPMENT BANK (2024)

Strategy Document: Framework to Support Populations in Situations of Fragility, Conflict, and Criminal Violence, 2024–2027

Focus. This framework establishes an organization-wide approach to working effectively in fragility, conflict, and criminal violence (FCCV) contexts. It provides guidance for adapting operations to address FCCV, emphasizing flexibility and contextualization.

Tools. The framework commits to developing new risk assessment tools for FCCV pockets and high-risk territories, including **political-economy analysis** and **fragility and resilience assessments.**

Funding and Support. The **People Strategy 2022–2027** prioritizes fragile contexts as one of five focus areas. It introduces measures to recruit and develop specialized skills, tailor recruitment processes, and build a talent pipeline for FCCV settings.

Principles of Engagement

- **Stay engaged** during crises, leveraging partnerships when direct presence is impossible.
- **Conflict sensitivity** to avoid reinforcing exclusion or shifting power dynamics.
- **Contextualized approaches** tailored to territorial realities.
- **Human rights focus**, addressing exclusion and inequality as drivers of fragility.
- **Local ownership** through participatory processes with state and non-state actors.
- **Institutional capacity building**, targeting legitimacy and cross-institutional effectiveness.
- **Private sector engagement** to foster jobs and markets in a conflict-sensitive manner.
- **Adaptability and learning**, embracing failure and accelerating iterative learning through monitoring and knowledge sharing.

Key Features

- **Classification methodology** for FCCV-affected countries and subnational hotspots, recognizing that violence in Latin America and the Caribbean is concentrated in specific areas rather than nationwide.
- **Focus on criminal violence**, the leading cause of fragility in the region, driven by organized crime and its feedback loops with instability.
- **Adaptive implementation**, emphasizing learning from failure and course correction.

Pillars

- **Applied knowledge agenda** – Close data gaps, identify FCCV pockets, develop risk assessment tools, and share insights to strengthen understanding.
- **Essential areas of support** – Prioritize institutional strengthening for better service delivery and address risk factors linked to criminal violence and conflict.
- **Strategic and operational adaptation** – Increase flexibility, accountability, and implementation capacity by tailoring processes to FCCV contexts while adhering to bank policies.

ISLAMIC DEVELOPMENT BANK (2019)

Strategy Document: Islamic Development Bank Fragility and Resilience Policy

Focus. The policy provides strategic direction for the Islamic Development Bank (IsDB) in addressing fragility and building resilience in member countries. It aims to strengthen institutions, promote social cohesion, and support sustainable development by tackling drivers of fragility such as exclusion, marginalization, and unequal development. A key emphasis is on prevention and bridging the gap between humanitarian relief and long-term development through partnerships.

Tools

- **Fragility and Resilience Risk Analysis**
- **Transition Management and Mitigation Strategy**
- **Resilience and Recovery Plan**
- **Joint Damage and Needs Assessment**

Principles of Engagement

- **Country ownership** – Align interventions with national development plans and priorities.
- **Selectivity** – Focus on areas where IsDB has comparative advantage.
- **Adaptability** – Tailor processes and guidelines to fragile contexts.
- **Solidarity** – Uphold the principle of alleviating human suffering.
- **Context and conflict sensitivity** – Ensure interventions are informed by local dynamics and avoid negative impacts.
- **Partnerships** – Coordinate with other actors to reduce duplication, share risks, and maximize synergies.

Key Features. The policy applies across all stages of conflict—before, during, and after—recognizing that these stages may overlap or occur simultaneously. It adopts a comprehensive approach to resilience-building and peace-building.

Pillars

- **Investing in prevention –** Promote inclusive growth, equity, and institutional strengthening to reduce fragility risks. Conflict sensitivity and prevention will be mainstreamed into country strategies, programs, and projects through **fragility and resilience risk analyses**.
- **Transitioning from relief to development –** Maintain engagement during conflict by bridging humanitarian assistance with development interventions that support economic recovery. A conflict monitoring mechanism guides investment decisions as conditions evolve.
- **Supporting recovery and resilience –** Rebuild four types of capital affected by conflict:
    - **Physical** – Infrastructure and trade
    - **Financial** – Access to resources
    - **Human** – Skills and education
    - **Social** – Trust in institutions and social cohesion

  Recovery efforts will include a resilience and recovery plan and post-conflict peace-building activities informed by **Joint Damage and Needs Assessment** findings.

- **Mobilizing resources for resilience.** Leverage IsDB's resources through partnerships, decentralized decision-making, and participatory platforms to enhance knowledge sharing, innovation, and coordination.

WORLD BANK GROUP (2020)

Strategy Document: World Bank Group Strategy for Fragility, Conflict, and Violence 2020–2025

Focus. The objective of this strategy, which is based on the twin goals of ending extreme poverty and boosting shared prosperity, is to enhance support to countries addressing the drivers and impacts of fragility, conflict, and violence and strengthening resilience, while looking at prevention.

Tool. Risk and Resilience Assessments

Funding and Support

- International Development Association (IDA)19: $21 billion, of which $18.7 billion is for countries impacted by fragility, conflict, and violence and $2.2 billion is for host communities and refugees
- International Finance Corporation and Multilateral Investment Guarantee Agency to significantly increase support ($2.5 billion window)

Strategy Approach. The strategy is structured around a set of guiding principles and four pillars, on the essential premise that, given the diversity of fragility, conflict, and violence challenges, there can be no one-size-fits-all approach. It covers eight dimensions of operationalization. Countries are classified based on the nature and severity of the issues they face, using two categories: institutional and social fragility, and violent conflict. The strategy identifies climate change, demographic challenges, gender inequalities, digital transformation, and illicit trafficking as drivers and multipliers of fragility and conflict.

Principles of Engagement

- Differentiation – Given interventions must be tailored to the drivers of fragility and conflict and fragile and conflict-affected situations require higher investments in data and analytics, security and staff welfare, on-the-ground presence, collaboration and coordination, and implementation.
- Inclusion – Through the pursuit of a people-centric approach that leaves no one behind. Youth and women are identified as key agents of change who can be mobilized to build resilience and peace.
- Legitimacy, transparency and accountability – With a long-term focus on the capacity of core government institutions.
- Scaling up private sector solutions for impact – Including by expanding the scope for simplified procedures and expanding risk mitigation approaches.

Pillars

- **Preventing violent conflict and interpersonal violence** – Addressing the key drivers of fragility and strengthening resilience factors, including by addressing gender inequality.
- **Remaining engaged during crises and active conflicts** – Engaging across the humanitarian–development–peace nexus. Undertaking assessment and due diligence to determine which situations warrant engagement during crises and open conflicts, considering the unique benefits and value that the World Bank Group can add.
- **Helping countries transition out of fragility** – Engaging with a broad range of actors and considering the government's capacity and strength of its social contract with citizens, to support countries to not relapse into violent conflict.
- **Mitigating the spillovers of fragility, conflict, and violence** – Interventions to address fragility, conflict, and violence should be paired with interventions that foster and protect human capital, adapting operations to the needs of at-risk groups that suffer disproportionately from the economic disruption of conflict.

Appendix 5

ASIAN DEVELOPMENT FUND GRANTS AND CONCESSIONAL LENDING

The Asian Development Fund (ADF) has been the Asian Development Bank's primary source of financing for its developing member countries (DMCs) classified as fragile and conflict-affected situations (FCAS) and small island developing states (SIDS).[1] ADF's evolution, including its resource allocation and windows for specific needs, reflects and responds to the unique needs and circumstances of FCAS and SIDS. ADF 14, the 13th replenishment of the fund, will support grant operations during 2025–2028 and further prioritizes support for the poorest and most vulnerable countries with a heavy emphasis on FCAS and SIDS.

ADB provides concessional assistance to its eligible DMCs to (i) finance targeted and tailored solutions for its poorest and most vulnerable DMCs that do not have the capacity to service external loans even on concessional terms, particularly those classified as FCAS and SIDS; (ii) support DMCs in pursuing thematic priorities, including climate action, regional cooperation and integration, and regional public goods, and achieving the Sustainable Development Goal (SDG) 5, which aims to achieve gender equality and empower all women and girls by 2030; (iii) leverage essential and urgent support for DMCs in crisis; and (iv) contribute to knowledge transfer and capacity development.

Concessional assistance, through ADF grants and concessional ordinary capital resources (OCR) lending (COL), is available to ADB DMCs classified as group A or group B.[2] For group A countries, eligibility for ADF grant and COL country allocations is determined by the risk of debt distress.[3] Table A3.1 shows the classification of DMCs that are eligible for ADF and COL as of 1 January 2026.

The ADF 14 Strategic Directions and Resource Allocation Framework

During the ADF 14 negotiations donors agreed on a total replenishment of $5.0 billion for the period 2025–2028.[4] This includes just under $4.0 billion for ADF grant financing and an allocation of approximately $560 million for ADB's Technical Assistance Special Fund (TASF) 8 (Figure A5.1).[5]

The ADF 14 resource allocation framework will continue to adopt a two-pillar system, consisting of country- and theme-based components. Revisions to improve the ADF's responsiveness, implementation efficiency, and effectiveness of resource allocation include:

(i) adjustments to the economic vulnerability premium (EVP), with the introduction of an allocation formula with a performance-based element to strengthen

1 A revised FCAS classification is a Management tool and does not create or modify eligibility for financial resources, unless separately approved in ADF policies.

2 ADB uses a three-tier DMC classification system: groups A, B, and C. Classification is determined by two key criteria: gross national income per capita (Atlas method) and creditworthiness. Group A countries are DMCs lacking creditworthiness. Group B countries are those with limited creditworthiness. Group C countries have adequate creditworthiness and per capita incomes exceeding the operational cut-off of the World Bank's International Development Association. Access to ADF grants and COL for group A countries is determined by the risk of debt distress. ADF grants are also provided to support thematic priorities. Group B countries have access to COL and regular OCR lending. Group C countries have access to regular OCR lending.

3 ADB. 2024. Concessional Assistance Policy for the ADF 14 Period: Policy Paper.

4 ADB. 2024. *Asian Development Fund 14 Donors' Report.*

5 The ADF 14 financing requirements also include $449 million for administrative expenses.

Table A5.1: 2026 Classification of ADB Developing Member Countries

Group A: Concessional Assistance Only (access to ADF grant and COL country allocations, and TASF)				Group B
ADF-Only	ADF Blend	COL-Only	IDA Gap	OCR Blend
(access to 100% ADF grant country allocations)	(access to 50% ADF grant country allocations)	(access to COL; no ADF grant country allocations)	(access to COL; no ADF grant country allocations)	(access to COL, regular OCR, and TASF)
At high-risk of debt distress	At moderate risk of debt distress	At low-risk of debt distress		
Afghanistan f Kiribati f s Maldives s Tajikistan Tonga s Tuvalu f s	Bhutan Federated States of Micronesia f s Marshall Islands f s Nauru f s Samoa s Vanuatu f s	Myanmar f Nepal Solomon Islands f s	Cambodia Kyrgyz Republic Lao People's Democratic Republic f	Bangladesh Cook Islands s Fiji s Mongolia Niue f s Pakistan Palau s Papua New Guinea f s Sri Lanka Timor-Leste f s Uzbekistan

f = FCAS s =SIDS

ADF = Asian Development Fund, COL = concessional ordinary capital resources lending, FCAS = fragile and conflict-affected situations, IDA = International Development Association, OCR = ordinary capital resources, SIDS = small island developing states, TASF = Technical Assistance Special Fund.

Notes:

1. IDA gap countries are group A countries (except small states, including SIDS) that have had gross national income per capita above the operational cutoff for IDA eligibility for more than 2 consecutive years and are assessed as a gap country by IDA. As of 1 July 2024, the operational cutoff was $1,335 (2023 prices), estimated using the Atlas method.
2. Afghanistan and Myanmar are suspended from the regular country allocation framework in the ADF 14 period (2025–2028) while ADB's regular operations in the countries are on hold. Classification is based on the latest publicly available International Monetary Fund and/or World Bank debt sustainability analysis.
3. The financing terms for Maldives have been hardened to COL terms since 2023 with 20% set aside from the performance-based allocation (50% grant, 50% COL in 2023–2024, and 100% COL in 2025–2026), due to repeated breaches of the requirement of no new non-concessional borrowing under the Sustainable Development Finance Policy.
4. Group B countries have access to ADF grants on a selective basis.

Source: ADB.

Figure A5.1: Asian Development Fund 14 Resource Allocation Framework

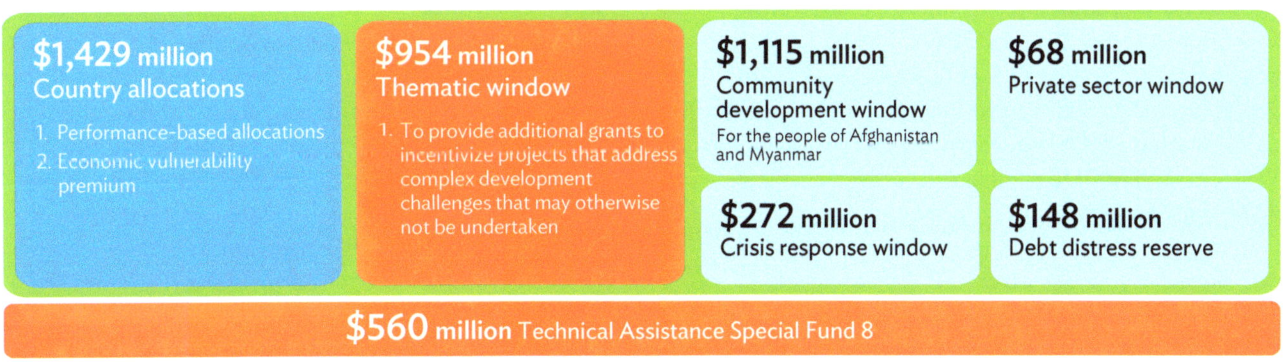

Source: ADB.

performance incentives, and the extension of a COL EVP to all COL-eligible SIDS;

(ii) an expanded thematic window (formerly the thematic pool) with increased resources allocated primarily to the climate change adaptation and disaster risk reduction strategic area, with smaller increases for fostering regional cooperation and integration, including the provision of regional public goods, and for the SDG5 transformative gender agenda; and an increase in the cap for group B countries to 15% of window resources;

(iii) added flexibility to allow the crisis response window (formerly the expanded disaster and pandemic response facility) to fund contingent disaster financing and other ex-ante disaster risk financing instruments in eligible DMCs;

(iv) introduction of a community development window for the people of Afghanistan[6] and Myanmar;[7] and

(v) expansion of eligibility for the private sector window to group B SIDS.

Additionally, donors requested that ADF 14 elevate crosscutting strategic issues. These include addressing inequalities, strengthening domestic resource mobilization, improving food security, fostering digital transformation, and promoting regional infrastructure connectivity. Lastly, through TASF 8, ADB will ensure that the poorest and most vulnerable DMCs receive adequate technical assistance (TA) resources by prioritizing allocations for FCAS, SIDS, and remaining group A countries.

FCAS- and SIDS-Relevant Components of the ADF 14 Framework

The ADF 14 resource allocation framework includes specific policy commitments related to ADB's support for FCAS-classified DMCs and SIDS. These commitments specify that (i) at least 32.5% of committed ADF 14 grants by volume will support SIDS and (ii) at least 40.0% of committed ADF 14 grants (by volume) will support FCAS-classified DMCs. Table A5.2 provides indicative ADF 14 allocations.

EVP for SIDS. In ADF 14, the EVP originally introduced in ADF 13 to provide additional grant resources to eligible SIDS is expanded, and COL resources for eligible SIDS are augmented. The EVP is calibrated based on (i) vulnerability, as measured by the United Nations Economic and Environmental Vulnerability Index, and (ii) the quality of policies and institutions, as measured by country performance assessments ratings.

Community Development Window for the People of Afghanistan and Myanmar. This window enables dedicated support for the people of countries in protracted crises, specifically for operations that support basic human needs and sustainable livelihoods development. Support from this window is in lieu of regular ADF grant and COL country allocations to Afghanistan (footnote 6) and Myanmar (footnote 7), which will be suspended while ADB's regular assistance to the countries is on hold. In addition to operations in Afghanistan and Myanmar, projects addressing the needs of displaced people from Myanmar in Bangladesh are eligible for support.

Thematic Window. Through the provision of additional grant resources, the thematic window under ADF 14 incentivizes governments to finance projects that have large development impact but low financial returns and/or projects in areas that generate positive externalities and regional spillovers. Specific strategic areas for the thematic window include: (i) supporting climate change adaptation and disaster risk reduction, (ii) fostering regional cooperation and integration, including the provision of regional public goods, and (iii) achieving the transformative gender agenda of SDG 5. FCAS-classified and SIDS DMCs have preferential access to thematic window resources.

Crisis Response Window. Provides timely financing to cover immediate needs in the aftermath of disasters triggered by natural hazards, large cross-border movements of displaced people, and public health emergencies. Contingent disaster financing instruments, and potentially other ex ante disaster risk financing instruments, are eligible for support.

[6] ADB placed its regular assistance to Afghanistan on hold effective 15 August 2021, with ADB providing support for basic human needs through United Nations agencies.

[7] Effective 1 February 2021, ADB placed a temporary hold on sovereign project disbursements and new contracts in Myanmar.

Table A5.2: Asian Development Fund 14 Indicative Allocations

Item			Amount ($ million)
Country allocation			1,429
	Of which:	Performance-based allocation	873
		Economic vulnerability premium	556
Community Development Window for the People of Afghanistan and Myanmar			1,115
Thematic Window			954
Crisis Response Window			272
Private Sector Window			68
Debt Distress Reserve			148
Total ADF grants			**3,986**
Memorandum items:			
Fragile and conflict-affected situations			**1,594**
Small island developing states			**1,295**

ADF = Asian Development Fund.

Notes:

1. Allocations are indicative and subject to change. Per the Concessional Assistance Policy for the ADF 14 Period, country allocations of ADF and concessional ordinary capital resources lending are allocated for the 4-year ADF cycle with annual updates that include annual resource adjustments across countries.
2. Numbers may not sum precisely because of rounding.

Source: ADB.

Private Sector Window. The private sector window supports a differentiated approach to stimulating private sector development, particularly in SIDS. Grants are provided for the economic viability and bankability of ADB-financed projects that may not proceed otherwise on a purely commercial basis. Solutions offered include local currency loans, blended finance, and loan guarantees. Support is available to Group A DMCs and Group B SIDS.

TASF 8. TASF supports TA as the primary nonlending instrument for delivering assistance to DMCs, while prioritizing allocations for FCAS-classified and SIDS DMCs. TASF 8 supports project preparation and implementation across sectors, along with high-quality knowledge solutions and policy advice. A dedicated set-aside also promotes debt management and sustainability in concessional assistance-eligible DMCs, including by supporting the implementation of policy actions under the Sustainable Development Finance Policy. Sufficient TASF resources build a pipeline of transformative and high-quality projects and also enhance project implementation and monitoring. TA plays an important role in focusing operations on developing regional and global public goods. TA can also promote private sector engagement and improve the conditions for private capital mobilization and catalyzation. Further, TA allows ADB to add value across the strategic focus areas.

Appendix 6

KEY TAKEAWAYS OF DESK REVIEW AND CONSULTATIONS INFORMING ACTION PLAN, 2026–2030

Refinement and clarification are needed in four key areas. The desk review encompassed independent evaluations, policy documents, and portfolio performance reviews. While Action Plan, 2026–2030 introduces refinements in implementation, it does not alter the institutional commitments or principles established under the 2021 Fragile and Conflict-Affected Situations (FCAS) and Small Island Developing States (SIDS) Approach. The desk review revealed four key areas to address and improve in Action Plan, 2026–2030. First, ADB's FCAS-classification system is criticized for its national-level binary structure of a developing member country (DMCs) as either FCAS or non-FCAS. This leads to three weaknesses: (i) ADB's differentiated approaches are not strictly applied to subnational conflicts in non-FCAS classified DMCs; (ii) the current system does not adequately reflect the full spectrum of resilience, including both strengths and weaknesses across multiple dimensions; and (iii) data do not capture cross-border regional spillover effects into non-FCAS classified countries, such as refugee movements.[1] Fragility and conflict are better understood as a spectrum, and country performance assessment scores used for classification may miss key risks for operations. The new classification system incorporates multidimensional, dynamic, and spectrum-based approaches.

The second key finding was that ADB's differentiated approach to FCAS and SIDS lacks operational clarity, unlike those at other multilateral development banks, which have more defined frameworks addressing fragility across various levels and phases of crisis and describe different presentations of fragility. The third finding was that fragility and resilience assessments (FRAs), which shape each country partnership strategy for FCAS-classified DMCs and SIDS, are essential but require more targeted and impactful content to be operationally relevant. Fourth, each ADB country partnership strategy is constrained by templates that limit in-depth discussion of vulnerability, fragility, and resilience, despite staff recognizing the need for stronger diagnostics and dissemination of diagnostics.

ADB staff praised increased visibility but called for further differentiation. Across consultations, staff said that the FCAS and SIDS Approach has succeeded in increasing the visibility of unique FCAS and SIDS contexts and the need for differentiated approaches.[2] However, multiple staff stakeholders voiced that the definition of differentiated approaches remains unclear. They also stressed that processes in FCAS and SIDS still largely mirror those for larger DMCs and that differentiated approaches, when they exist, are inconsistently applied.

---

1 The converse is also true, where investment in a non-FCAS classified country neighboring an FCAS-classified country could have positive spillovers to an FCAS country.

2 Between early August 2025 and January 2026, staff from ADB's Fragility and Engagement Division met over 110 staff in more than 35 consultations across ADB, including Sectors Departments, themes, procurement, financial management, private sector operations, and regional departments. They discussed both the implementation of the FSA to date as well as how it needs to adapt to continue to serve DMCs. Feedback included how staff understand and apply differentiated approaches in their work, how updated business processes have served them to date, how they perceive capacity development efforts to have affected ADB's work in FCAS and SIDS contexts, and how they have experienced greater efforts to improve understanding of DMC contexts.

Procurement, financial management, and project readiness remain overly complex, with small projects in FCAS and SIDS generally subject to the same documentation, indicators, and safeguards as large-scale operations.[3] This slows delivery and strains already stretched resident missions and implementing agencies.

While initiatives like Wayfinder[4] and increased outposting are promising, stakeholders noted a persistent gap between policy intentions and operational realities, with staff and clients still navigating lengthy procedures and unclear incentives. Institutional capacity concerns were repeatedly raised, including staffing gaps, staff location, reliance on junior staff, limited cultural preparation and contextual knowledge, weak sustainability planning, and a limited pool of consultants with FCAS and SIDS expertise and country knowledge for extended assignments. Analytical and diagnostic work is valued but could be more accessible, timely, and applicable.

Further progress on action plan pillars is needed. Stakeholders recommended more ambitious, practical steps to realize differentiated approaches. Common suggestions included (i) further tailoring of procurement, financial management, and environmental and social safeguards procedures for FCAS and SIDS, (ii) adjusting project processing thresholds and approval levels for very small projects, and (iii) preparing design and monitoring frameworks, indicators, and evaluations suited to FCAS and SIDS contexts that will improve results measurement. ADB's institutional capacity was frequently raised by stakeholders, who recommended capacity should be strengthened by deploying more senior and experienced staff, expanding outposting, providing context-specific induction training, and expanding the ADB–World Bank roster of consulting firms beyond detailed design and construction supervision and developing framework agreements with individual consultants in FCAS and SIDS. Knowledge retention and peer networks should be institutionalized to mitigate knowledge and relationship networks loss from staff turnover in ADB and executing and implementing agencies. This would address the issue of successful differentiated approaches being developed but not implemented across the board, as the knowledge is held by a limited number of individuals. On analytics, stakeholders recommended that FRAs and related analytics should be concise, operationally relevant, and feed directly into project design and risk management. Finally, stakeholders stressed the need to align incentives, resource allocations, and performance frameworks in ADB, noting the higher transaction costs of FCAS and SIDS operations.

Additional and new operational flexibilities are required. Moreover, project officers called for further flexibilities, especially in procurement, financial management, and safeguards, particularly for small, low-value projects presenting minimal risk. In terms of capacity, the new operating model resulted in staff movements where many staff without prior experience in FCAS-SIDS contexts have been assigned to handle projects in FCAS-classified DMCs which present completely different challenges. This necessitates boosting capacity to familiarize project officers with differentiated approaches, including new country directors. While operations departments value the importance of FRAs, they requested more guidance on applying their findings and resilience actions during project preparation.

Constituencies emphasized more transformative approaches. Consultations with Board members emphasized the need for a transformative approach that addresses the root causes of fragility and delivers tangible development impact in FCAS and SIDS.[5] Members highlighted that, despite longstanding efforts, persistent structural issues such as weak governance, limited institutional capacity, and economic vulnerability remain. They called for Action Plan, 2026–2030 to move beyond process orientation and focus on real development results, urging clearer priorities, boundaries, and a distinct value proposition for ADB in these contexts. Strong country ownership was underscored as essential for

3 The new Environmental and Social Framework gives more flexibility to the application of safeguards requirements for low to moderate risk projects and under full implementation should yield more streamlined environmental and social due diligence approaches for such projects.

4 ADB. 2025. *ADB Wayfinder (Pacific) Program under the Enhanced Faster Approach to Small Nonsovereign Transactions Policy*.

5 This included an informal board session in November 2025 and bilateral meetings with constituencies.

effectiveness and sustainability, with requests for more demand-driven planning and deeper client consultation to ensure genuine buy-in from FCAS and SIDS DMCs.

Further, they advocated for more clearly articulated differentiated approaches, not just in business processes but also in portfolio design, thematic priorities, and operational instruments.

They stressed the importance of contextual responsiveness, especially distinguishing strategies for SIDS versus FCAS (in particular conflict-affected situations), and called for all ADB departments to reflect on how differentiated approaches could be applied in their respective areas of work. The need for a robust theory of change and results framework was also raised, with requests for clearer indicators, intermediate benchmarks, and alignment with Strategy 2030. Additionally, the importance of institutional responsiveness, integration with other ADB strategies, private sector development, regional cooperation, and updating the FCAS classification system to better capture varying degrees of fragility were highlighted. Lessons from FRAs, as well as the need to strengthen staff capacities and cultural competence, were also discussed as critical to improving ADB's impact in these challenging environments.

Partners encouraged stronger tailored support, coordination, and capacity development. Key takeaways emerged from consultations with officials from development partner organizations and DMC governments.[6] First, participants confirmed the growing and compounding factors that are driving fragility across the region and the important implications this has for development partners and DMCs to make more ambitious efforts on resilience-building. With some bilateral partners scaling back or refocusing their financing in key areas, the role and potential contribution of multilateral development banks become relatively more important. On the other hand, several development partners emphasized the critical importance of ADF; they reiterated that it must evolve to continue to reflect the needs of FCAS and SIDS. They noted the critical importance for all partners to differentiate how they work in FCAS and SIDS but also mentioned that this can be pursued through various methods across organizations. DMC officials expressed specific appreciation for ADB's continued efforts to tailor its business processes, build its internal capacity, and deepen its knowledge of DMCs. They also requested stronger support to develop the capabilities of their agencies that work with ADB and other major partners.

Partners and officials also affirmed the need to step up coordination and collaboration among major development partners, especially in the smaller FCAS and SIDS where coordination and implementation capacity remains very limited. Several partners noted the importance of strengthening the availability and capability of DMC-based consultants and contractors, as this is often a weak link in the design and delivery of major projects, particularly infrastructure. Widespread support was expressed for taking a long-term and more deliberate approach to building national capacities in key DMC executing and implementing agencies at the individual, system, and organizational levels.

6 Consultations were held with officials from development partners and DMCs, including Australia's Department of Foreign Affairs and Trade, the Japan International Cooperation Agency, the Marshall Islands, New Zealand Ministry of Foreign Affairs and Trade, Palau, Papua New Guinea, Secretariat of the Pacific Community, World Bank, and the US Office of Insular Affairs.

Appendix 7

ACTION PLAN ALIGNMENT WITH INSTITUTIONAL PRIORITIES

Strategy 2030 Midterm Review and differentiated approaches. The Strategy 2030 Midterm Review (MTR) recognizes the progress ADB has made on applying differentiated approaches in fragile and conflicted-affected situations (FCAS) and small island developing states (SIDS) contexts but notes a need to (i) address gaps in the application of key policies and business processes that constrain meaningful operationalization of differentiated approaches and (ii) firm up the understanding of differentiated approaches both strategically and operationally.[1] The MTR committed ADB to a new target for operations in FCAS and SIDS contexts, and ADB's Corporate Results Framework (CRF), 2025–2027 subsequently set a target for financing of FCAS and SIDS to increase from 4.4% to 7.5% by 2030.[2] This significant upscaling will require ADB to meaningfully operationalize differentiated approaches, not only to reach the financing target, but to ensure the effectiveness of increased ADB-financed operations. Action Plan, 2026–2030 recognizes the continued relevance of more flexible and responsive policies and procedures, strengthened institutional capacities, and enhanced understanding of developing member country (DMC) contexts to increase effective financing in FCAS and SIDS contexts. Accordingly, Action Plan, 2026–2030 maintains the original three pillars outlined in the FCAS and SIDS Approach, while also responding to ADB's strategic priorities and the need to meaningfully operationalize differentiated approaches through refreshed implementation actions.

Evolving institutional context. The Strategy 2030 MTR examines progress, identifies areas for change, and proposes a path for ADB's evolution to enable ADB to respond effectively to the scope and severity of development challenges facing Asia and the Pacific. The global development context and the conditions in which ADB operates have changed significantly since ADB approved Strategy 2030 in 2018, and FCAS-classified DMCs and SIDS have suffered disproportionate losses in gross domestic product and reduced growth forecasts as a result of the coronavirus disease pandemic and resultant cascading crises. To respond to these growing needs, the Strategy 2030 MTR calls urgently for ADB to update its vision, financial capacity, and operational approach.

Given that the Pacific is home to the largest share of SIDS in Asia and the Pacific, the unique needs of the Pacific are mainstreamed throughout Action Plan, 2026–2030. Both *Pillar 1 Improving responsiveness of standard ADB processes and procedures* and *Pillar 2 Increasing ADB's institutional capacity for operations in FCAS and SIDS contexts* are highly relevant to increasing effectiveness in the Pacific. The forthcoming Pacific Approach, 2026–2030, which will propose measures to support operations in 12 small Pacific DMCs, will build on Action Plan, 2026–2030 to further articulate specific actions to apply a differentiated approach in the Pacific. Pacific Approach, 2026–2030, currently under development, will be supported by pillar 3's enhanced analytics to understand DMC contexts as part of applying a differentiated approach to SIDS, with fragility and resilience assessments for all 12 Pacific small island states being developed to inform the approach.

Embedding five strategic focus areas in FCAS and SIDS operations. Strategy 2030 MTR identifies five strategic focus areas (SFAs) to guide ADB's decision-making and address the growing development challenges that

---

1 ADB. 2024. *Strategy 2030 Midterm Review: An Evolution Approach for the Asian Development Bank*.

2 ADB. 2024. *Steering ADB's Corporate Strategy to Success: Corporate Results Framework, 2025–2030*.

threaten ADB's vision for the region, with the rationale and priority focus areas outlined for each SFA. The relevance of each SFA and ADB's planned support for FCAS and SIDS contexts for each under Action Plan, 2026–2030 are outlined below. Although the five SFAs cut across the three pillars of Action Plan, 2026–2030, they are explicitly identified under *Key Action Area 3.2 Strengthen the strategic application and linkages of fragility and resilience assessments, in collaboration with a wide range of stakeholders and highlighting the five SFAs under the Strategy 2030 MTR.* This key action area will ensure the analytics and diagnostics that inform ADB's country partnership strategies incorporate a sophisticated understanding of how the SFAs intersect with vulnerability, fragility, and resilience dynamics in DMCs. The following also references key ADB policy architecture where applicable.

Strategic Focus Area 1 – Climate Action. This SFA establishes ADB's updated target to deliver more than $100 billion in cumulative climate finance (2019–2030), and for climate finance to reach 50% of the total committed financing volume, by 2030. It also includes increased commitment to operations supporting disaster risk management, and environment and nature. The SFA emphasizes two imperatives particularly relevant to the climate–fragility nexus: (i) the need to champion a socially just transition and reduce inequality, and (ii) a commitment to foster climate and disaster resilience and enhance ADB's work in response to growing risks. The need for a differentiated approach to climate change action is established in ADB's Climate Change Action Plan, 2023–2030, given that vulnerability and fragility in FCAS-classified DMCs and SIDS stem from heightened exposure to risk and insufficient coping capacity to manage, absorb, or mitigate it.[3] FCAS-classified DMCs face additional constraints in mobilizing external climate finance and domestic resources for climate action compared to non-FCAS classified DMCs, requiring more targeted support and funding modalities.[4] Additionally, evidence-based climate decision-making in FCAS and SIDS contexts requires special consideration, given constraints in available and reliable data. Action Plan, 2026–2030 responds to this SFA and aligns to ADB's Climate Change Action Plan, 2023–2030 by mainstreaming climate throughout *Pillar 3 Enhancing understanding of DMC contexts*, effectively building the evidence base for informed decision-making on the climate–fragility nexus.

Strategic Focus Area 2 – Private Sector Development. This SFA establishes that private sector development (PSD) and greater private investment are essential to meet significant development needs. PSD across ADB's DMCs is challenged by market failures and legal and regulatory gaps, as well as underdeveloped infrastructure, particularly in FCAS and SIDS contexts, which face higher risk profiles, limited access to finance, geographic remoteness, and a lack of economies of scale. ADB's new operating model introduced the "*PSD shift*" to promote a bank-wide holistic approach in support of its DMCs to enhance enabling environments and achieve greater private sector participation and investment. The implementation of the shift will be based on policy and strategy documents that have provided priority and direction for PSD, including the PSD-related targets set within ADB's CRF, 2025–2030: (i) 40% of annual committed sovereign loan operations are to contribute meaningfully to PSD, and (ii) $13.0 billion of financing for private investment is to be committed and/or mobilized annually by 2030. ADB has made concrete efforts toward catalyzing PSD in FCAS and SIDS contexts through the introduction of policies, processes, targets, and financial instruments. To realize this ambition, ADB also set a target under the CRF of 50% of nonsovereign operations taking place in frontier economies by 2030,[5] which will contribute to incentivizing nonsovereign operations in FCAS and SIDS contexts.[6] Building on an *Enhanced Faster Approach to Small Nonsovereign Transactions*[7] and designed to contribute to the new CRF target,

3 ADB. 2023. *Climate Change Action Plan 2023–2030*.

4 The target is for 7.5% of total commitments (sovereign and nonsovereign) for FCAS and SIDS by 2030.

5 Frontier economies refer to group A or B countries (excluding India), SIDS, and FCAS-classified countries. ADB uses a three-tier DMC classification system: groups A, B, and C. Classification is determined by two key criteria: gross national income per capita (Atlas method) and creditworthiness. Group A countries are DMCs lacking creditworthiness. Group B countries are those with limited creditworthiness. Group C countries have adequate creditworthiness and per capita incomes exceeding the operational cut-off of the World Bank's International Development Association.

6 The target is for 50% of committed nonsovereign operations in frontier economies, which includes FCAS and SIDS.

7 ADB. 2022. *Enhanced Faster Approach to Small Nonsovereign Transactions*.

ADB introduced the ADB Wayfinder (Pacific) Program to enhance ADB's ability to originate, process, and monitor nonsovereign transactions in the Pacific SIDS.[8] ADB Frontier was also launched to catalyze the growth of small and medium-sized enterprises and support market development in SIDS and FCAS contexts.[9] Finally, the addition of a country PSD annex in each country partnership strategy is an additional and important lever to enhance understanding of the intersection between PSD, fragility, and resilience in FCAS and SIDS contexts, therefore enabling solutions to attract private sector investment to higher-risk contexts. Reflecting the importance of this SFA, Action Plan 2026–2030 not only mainstreams consideration of nonsovereign operations under *Pillar 1 Improving responsiveness of standard ADB processes and procedures*, but also includes scope to build institutional capacities under Pillar 2 and enhance analytics under Pillar 3.

Strategic Focus Area 3 – Regional Cooperation and Public Goods. This SFA recognizes the evolving and increasingly complex landscape for regional cooperation and integration in Asia and the Pacific, given interconnected trends in financial and digital connectivity, including a reliance on regional and international payment systems, and environmental cooperation. To enable increased delivery of critical regional public goods ADB must deliver an enhanced approach to regional cooperation and public goods. Regional cooperation and public goods considerations for FCAS and SIDS contexts include the causal relationship between increased economic interdependence and reduced interstate conflict and transborder climate and environmental challenges such as sea-level rise, ocean pollution, and glacial melt.[10] Action Plan, 2026–2030 includes the flexibility for demand-driven support on regional cooperation and integration in FCAS and SIDS contexts across ADB, including through institutional capacity building.

Strategic Focus Area 4 – Digital Transformation. This SFA urges ADB to accelerate its work, particularly on digital infrastructure and governance, to meet rapidly growing client demand for digital solutions that can drive economic growth in Asia and the Pacific. ADB will prepare a new digital transformation action plan and commits to grow digital transformation operations year on year. Particular risks in FCAS and SIDS contexts include low institutional readiness and capacities to guard against cyberattacks, limited resources for the sustainable operational maintenance of digital infrastructure, potential deepening of the urban–rural or inner–outer island divide given higher costs in accessing digital networks, and fragility risks from job displacement and brain drain. As a result, ADB will need to strengthen its capabilities to provide policy advice and process digital transformation operations in FCAS and SIDS contexts, with consideration for multidimensional risk and resilience factors and potential interactions between digital transformation and the underlying drivers of fragility and conflict. Action Plan, 2026–2030 will support ADB's capacities to provide policy advice and develop risk-informed digital transformation operations primarily underneath *Pillar 3 Enhancing understanding of DMC contexts*.

[8] ADB. 2025. ADB Wayfinder (Pacific) Program under the Enhanced Faster Approach to Small Nonsovereign Transactions Policy.
[9] ADB. 2024. ADB Frontier Seed (Pacific).
[10] J.R. Oneal, and B. Russett. 1999. Assessing the Liberal Peace with Alternative Specifications: Trade Still Reduces Conflict. *Journal of Peace Research*. 36 (4). pp. 423–442.

Appendix 8

RESULTS FRAMEWORK INDICATORS FOR MONITORING

The Fragile and Conflict-Affected Situations (FCAS) and Small Island Developing States (SIDS) Approach (FSA) Results Framework consists of 19 results indicators and 18 actions of Action Plan, 2026–2030. These results indicators are based on the results framework and tracking indicators of ADB's Corporate Results Framework, 2025–2030,[1] disaggregated for FCAS-classified developing member countries (DMCs) and SIDS. The action trackers monitor the specific actions under the key action areas of Action Plan, 2026–2030.

Level 1 outcome-level indicators measure the contribution of FCAS and SIDS operations to ADB's development results. These include indicators measuring the number of people with improved standards of living, people benefiting from improved services (e.g., health, education, social protection, infrastructure, financial, economic), women and girls benefiting from greater gender equality, people with strengthened climate and disaster resilience, jobs generated, and businesses and institutions with improved service delivery. These indicators link to the top of the theory of change (TOC), which predicts improved livelihoods, inclusiveness, and resilience in FCAS and SIDS, which in turn will result in sustainable development.

Level 2 indicators measure ADB commitments in the strategic focus areas of the Strategy 2030 Midterm Review: resilience and empowerment, private sector development, climate action, regional cooperation and public goods, and digital transformation.[2] Indicators measuring the success rates of completed sovereign and nonsovereign operations in FCAS-classified DMCs and SIDS are also part of Level 2 indicators. These indicators connect with the middle level of the TOC, improved performance of ADB operations in FCAS and SIDS.

Level 3 indicators measure the performance of ongoing operations as well as human resources dedicated to FCAS–SIDS. These indicators are supported by the action trackers of Action Plan, 2026–2030, which promote differentiated approaches by improving responsiveness of processes, increasing institutional capacity, and enhancing understanding of DMC contexts. They align with the bottom level of the TOC, increased use of differentiated approaches in ADB operations in FCAS and SIDS. The figure illustrates the relationships among these levels of indicators.

1 ADB. 2024. *Steering ADB's Corporate Strategy to Success: Corporate Results Framework, 2025–2030*.

2 ADB. 2024. *Summary of Midterm Review: Fragile and Conflict-Affected Situations and Small Island Developing States Approach*.

Figure A8.1: ADB Corporate Results Framework Indicators Related to FCAS–SIDS

SUSTAINABLE DEVELOPMENT

↑

1. Improved livelihoods, inclusiveness, and resilience in FCAS and SIDS

- 1.A People in poverty and vulnerable situations with improved standards of living (number, achievement rate)
- 1.B People benefiting from improved health services, education services, or social protection (number, achievement rate)
- 1.C People benefiting from improved infrastructure, financial, and economic services (number, achievement rate)
- 1.D Women and girls benefiting from greater gender equality (number, achievement rate)
- 1.E People with strengthened climate and disaster resilience (number, achievement rate)
- 1.F Jobs generated (number, achievement rate)
- 1.G Businesses and public institutions with improved service delivery and financial stability (number, achievement rate)

↑

2. Improved performance of ADB operations in FCAS and SIDS

- 2.A Financing for FCAS and SIDS (% of $, sovereign and nonsovereign operations)
- 2.B Committed operations contributing to private sector development in FCAS and SIDS (% of #, sovereign)
- 2.C Financing for climate action in FCAS and SIDS (% of $, sovereign and nonsovereign operations)
- 2.D Committed operations supporting regional cooperation and integration in FCAS and SIDS (% of #, sovereign and nonsovereign operations)
- 2.E Committed operations supporting digital transformation in FCAS and SIDS (% of #, sovereign and nonsovereign operations)
- 2.F Completed operations rated successful (% of #, sovereign)
- 2.G Completed operations rated successful (% of #, nonsovereign)

↑

3. Increased use of differentiated approaches in ADB operations in FCAS and SIDS

- 3.A Operations that are implementation-ready before approval (% of #, sovereign)
- 3.B Operations under implementation at risk for four reporting periods or more (% of #, sovereign)
- 3.C Internationally and locally hired technical staff in FCAS and SIDS field offices (#, sovereign)
- 3.D Team leaders in the field for processing and implementation (% of #, sovereign)
- 3.E Achievement of knowledge program delivery in FCAS and SIDS as per regional work programs (% of #, sovereign)

FSA Action Plan (action tracker)
8 Key Action Areas
18 Actions

ADB = Asian Development Bank, FCAS = fragile and conflict-affected situations, FSA = FCAS and SIDS Approach, SIDS = small island developing states.

Note: The results indicators are disaggregated data for FCAS-SIDS based on broader ADB Corporate Results Framework indicators. Given the small number of projects in FCAS–SIDS, the FSA did not set baselines and targets. The indicators are for monitoring purposes only.

Source: ADB.

www.ingramcontent.com/pod-product-compliance
Lightning Source LLC
Chambersburg PA
CBHW041759220926
51847CB00014B/253
9789292778064